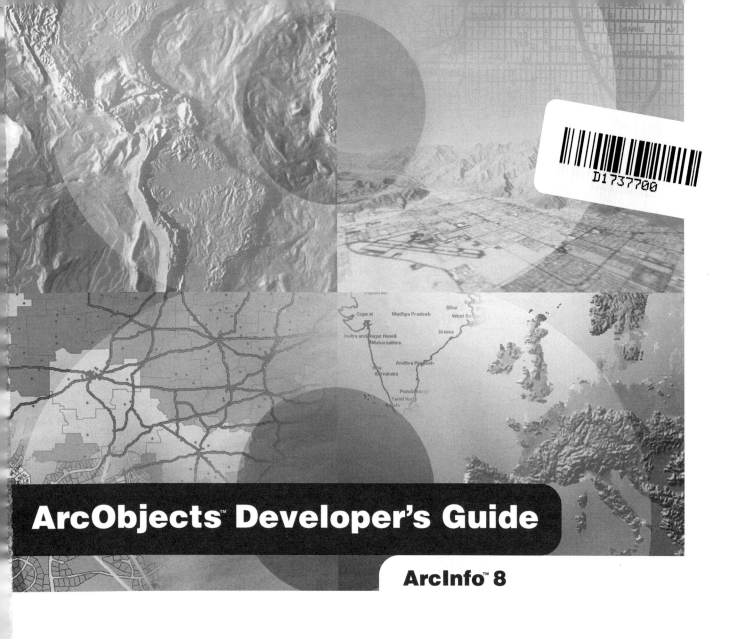

ArcObjects™ Developer's Guide

ArcInfo™ 8

Contents

Welcome to the ArcObjects Developer's Guide

Welcome to the *ArcObjects Developer's Guide*. This book will introduce you to the development tools and environment that are available for customizing, extending, and creating extensions for ESRI® end-user applications. This chapter briefly describes the following:

• The audience for this book

• The contents of the book; what's in each chapter

• How to get help

• How to get in touch with us at ESRI

Who this book is for

The *ArcObjects Developer's Guide* is for anyone who wants to learn the basic techniques and principles of customizing or adding functionality to the ArcInfo™ end-user applications by working graphically with the user interface or by referencing the ArcObjects™ object model in a development environment. This book assumes you have some familiarity with the end-user applications, ArcMap™ and ArcCatalog™, and have had some experience designing and implementing applications or additional functionality for another ESRI software program or other Microsoft® Windows®-based programs.

Microsoft Visual Basic® for Applications (VBA) is embedded in ArcInfo end-user applications; consequently, the majority of the code examples in this book are in Visual Basic. Expertise or even previous experience with VB is not a requirement. You'll find that you'll become productive quickly in Visual Basic's development environment. If you're a C++®; programmer, several examples in C++ are available in the *ArcObjects Developer Help* help file, and you can also learn from additional C++ code in Chapter 9 of this book.

What's in this book

Although you can read this book from start to finish, you'll likely use it more as a reference. Different readers, with different programming skills or interests, will no doubt take different routes through this book.

Begin learning how to customize ArcMap and ArcCatalog by reading Chapter 2, 'Quick-start tutorial'. This chapter shows you how quickly and easily you can change the way you can present the applications, add scripts, or create new components to distribute to others. The tutorial doesn't require extensive geographic data—you can use the geographic data that comes with the applications, or you can use your own data. Follow along step by step at your computer or read the tutorial without using your computer.

Chapter 3, 'Customizing ESRI applications graphically', covers how to customize the applications graphically. When you want to know how to do a particular task, just look it up in the table of contents or index. What you'll find is a concise, step-by-step description of how to complete the task.

Read the beginning sections of Chapter 4, 'Programming ESRI applications', to learn about the concepts and techniques that lie at the heart of developing with ESRI's Component Object Model (COM) based object model. It's recommended reading even if you've previously worked with Visual Basic or another application in which VBA is embedded.

If you haven't worked with Visual Basic for Applications before and want to understand more about working in the development environment embedded in ArcMap and ArcCatalog, read the remainder of Chapter 4.

Chapters 5 through 8 include detailed information that you can read if you want to learn more about the various sections of the ArcObjects object model. Each chapter provides conceptual descriptions of the relevant portions of the object model for the Customization Framework, ArcMap, ArcCatalog, and the Geodatabase, followed by illustrative code examples.

If you want to use Computer-Aided Software Engineering (CASE) tools to define custom features, create code to add custom behavior, and create geodatabase schema, follow the tutorial in Chapter 9, 'Working with CASE tools'. The tutorial requires Visio® Enterprise and Developer Studio 6.0. You should have familiarity with C++, ActiveX® Template Library (ATL), and COM.

Chapter 10 provides information about packaging and deploying extensions and add-ins for the ESRI applications.

If you're new to GIS and mapping, remember that you don't have to learn everything about geographic information systems, or for that matter, the entire ESRI Object Library, to get immediate results that your user community will appreciate. This book describes the development tasks—from the simplest graphic customization to a sophisticated use of the object library—that you'll perform.

If you prefer to jump right in and experiment on your own, you can start an application, go to the development environment and start to work with the object model, or load in one of the samples delivered with the applications.

Getting help

In addition to this book, you'll find that the online help for developers is a valuable resource for learning how to use the software. Online help is available for all the interfaces, coclasses, and enumerations of the ArcObjects object model. Learn how to get help in the Code Window of the Visual Basic Editor or the Object Browser in Chapter 2, 'Quick-start tutorial'. You can also view diagrams of the entire object model and make use of an extensive collection of samples by selecting *ArcObjects Developer Help* in the ArcInfo program group.

Contacting ESRI

If you need to contact ESRI for technical support, see the product registration and support card you received with your applications or refer to 'Obtaining technical support' in the Help system's Troubleshooting section. You can also visit ESRI on the Web at www.esri.com for more information.

Quick-start tutorial

2

This chapter contains a tutorial that will help you become familiar with the ESRI application developer experience. First, you'll see how to control the way ArcMap and ArcCatalog look by modifying the user interface graphically. Next, you'll use the development environment that's embedded in ESRI applications, Visual Basic for Applications (VBA), to create your own commands. At the end of the tutorial, you'll take a closer look at the ESRI Object Library and see how to create a COM component using Visual Basic.

This chapter and the rest of this book assume some familiarity with programming with Visual Basic and the terms used to describe it. Only key terms are described if necessary. A brief discussion of the embedded Visual Basic for Applications development environment appears in Chapter 4, 'Programming ESRI applications'. If you haven't worked with Visual Basic or VBA before, see the Microsoft Visual Basic online help.

Customizing the user interface

Getting started

Chapter 3, 'Customizing ESRI applications graphically', shows how to carry out many of the customization tasks you want to accomplish without writing a single line of code. This tutorial provides a quick, guided tour of some of those same key tasks; details and explanations are left for later so that you can start to work as quickly as possible.

1. To start this tutorial, click ArcMap in the Start menu's ArcInfo program group.

2. In the startup dialog, click Start using ArcMap.

3. Add some sample data or your own data to the map.

Moving and docking toolbars

You may find that you prefer to work with certain screen elements positioned in specific locations.

1. Click the move handle of a docked toolbar or the title bar on a floating toolbar.

   A *docked toolbar* is a toolbar that's attached to one edge of the program window. Its move handle is the vertical bar at its left-hand edge.

   A *floating toolbar* is not attached to an edge of the program window. If you work with ArcCatalog, you'll be able to control its toolbars using the same techniques as described below.

2. Drag the floating Tools toolbar and position it below the Standard toolbar.

You can ensure that the Tools toolbar will appear below the Standard toolbar by releasing its drag outline below and to the left of the move handle of the Standard toolbar.

3. Now dock the Tools toolbar at the bottom of the Application window by releasing its drag outline just above the status bar.

4. Drag the Tools toolbar to its original, floating position outside the Application window.

   If you release the toolbar at the inside edge of the application window, it will appear as a docked toolbar.

Showing and hiding the table of contents, status bar, and scroll bars

In addition to positioning its toolbars, you can control whether or not to display the ArcMap table of contents, status bar, and scroll bars. If you work with ArcCatalog, you'll be able to control its Catalog tree and status bar using the same techniques described below.

In the View menu, click the image next to the appropriate menu item to toggle the visible state of the object.

The View menu in ArcMap and ArcCatalog

You can also click the small buttons at the top of the table of contents or Catalog tree to contract, hide, and expand its window.

If you click the Hide Window button and want to show it again, use the View menu.

Showing and hiding toolbars

For some tasks you may find that specific toolbars are not needed or occupy screen real estate that you need for some other toolbar or purpose. Two of the techniques for showing and hiding toolbars are described below. You can perform the same operations in ArcCatalog.

1. In the View menu, choose Toolbars and then click off the check mark next to Tools.

2. In the View menu, choose Toolbars and then click on the check mark next to Editor.

3. Dismiss the Editor menu by clicking its close button on the right-hand side of its title bar.

Showing and hiding toolbars using the Customize dialog

1. In the Tools menu click Customize.

   The Customize dialog appears.

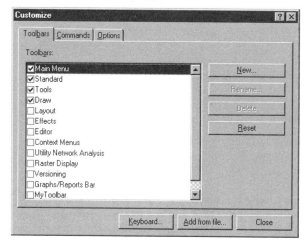

You can also double-click any unoccupied area of any toolbar to display the Customize dialog.

2. If it is not visible, click the Toolbars tab.

   The presence or absence of a check mark next to the toolbar name indicates its visible state, just as in the Toolbars submenu of the View menu.

3. Click the check mark of the Tools menu off and on.

Creating a new toolbar

1. In the Toolbars tab of the Customize dialog, click the New button.

2. In the dialog that appears, specify My Tools as the name of the new toolbar or use the default setting.

3. Store the toolbar in the document by changing the name of the Save in dropdown list from Normal.mxt to Untitled or the name of the current project.

4. Click OK.

   The newly created toolbar appears near the top of the application window.

Adding buttons to a toolbar

1. Make sure the toolbar you just created, My Tools, is visible.

2. If it is not visible, display the Customize dialog.

3. Click the Commands tab of the Customize dialog.

4. Select the Pan/Zoom category from the Categories list at the left of the dialog.

5. Scroll to the bottom of the Commands list at the right of the dialog.

6. Select the Zoom in command and drag it to the My Tools toolbar.

Release the command when the I-bar and + (plus sign) cursor appear.

7. Continue adding commands from the Pan/Zoom category until you have your own version of the built-in Tools toolbar.

Note that you'll have to switch to the Selection category and the Page Layout category to locate some of the other tools.

8. Resize the toolbar so that its width allows the display of two commands per row.

   Note that you can dock the toolbar or drag it to wherever you want such as any of the other toolbars.

Renaming a toolbar

1. In the Toolbars tab, select the name of the toolbar whose name you want to change.

   In this case, select My Tools.

2. Click the Rename button.

3. In the dialog that appears, specify My Own Tools as the new name.

   Note that you can only rename toolbars you've created.

4. Click OK.

   If you choose not to rename the toolbar, click Cancel.

Removing buttons from a toolbar

1. Make sure the toolbar you just renamed, My Own Tools, is visible.

2. If it is not visible, display the Customize dialog.

3. Drag the Fixed Zoom In, Fixed Zoom Out, Full Extent, Go Back to Previous Extent, Go to Next Extent, and Select Features buttons off the toolbar.

Even though you've removed the buttons from the toolbar, they are still available in the Customize dialog box.

Adding a menu to a toolbar

1. Make sure the toolbar named My Own Tools is visible.

2. If it is not visible, display the Customize dialog.

3. Click the Commands tab and choose the Menus category from the Categories list at the left-hand side of the dialog.

4. In the Commands list at the right-hand side of the dialog, choose Selection.

5. Drag and drop it to the right of the Zoom Out button on the My Own Tools toolbar.

6. In the Customize dialog, click Close.

7. Click Selection on the My Own Tools toolbar and note the menu that appears.

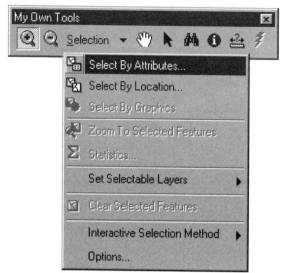

Saving changes to a template

You can save your work to a document or template. Changes saved to a document are specific to the document, whereas changes saved to a template will be reflected in all documents based on the template.

1. In the File menu, click Save As.

2. In the Save As dialog, navigate to the Templates folder of the <installation directory>\bin folder.

3. Click the Create New Folder button.

   Type a new name for the folder and then double-click it. You'll see the folder name as a tab the next time you create a document from a template.

4. Type the template name, choose ArcMap Templates (*.mxt), and then click Save.

Writing macros in VBA

VBA is embedded in ArcMap and ArcCatalog. You can use this interactive development environment to create macros to help you automate tasks you perform repeatedly or to extend the application's built-in functionality.

Creating a macro

With the Visual Basic Editor, you can edit macros, copy macros from one module to another, rename the modules that store the macros, or rename the macros.

1. In the Tools menu, select Macros and then Macros.

2. In the Macros dialog, type MyZoomIn in the Macro name text box and then click Create.

   The application creates a new module named NewMacros and stubs in the Sub procedure.

3. Enter the following code for MyZoomIn:

```
Sub MyZoomIn()
'
' macro: MyZoomIn
'
    Dim pDoc As IMxDocument
    Dim pEnv As IEnvelope
    Set pDoc = ThisDocument
    Set pEnv = pDoc.ActiveView.Extent
    pEnv.Expand 0.5, 0.5, True
    pDoc.ActiveView.Extent = pEnv
    pDoc.ActiveView.Refresh
End Sub
```

The first line of the macro declares a variable that represents the ArcMap document. At this point, we won't go into the coding techniques that are used with the ArcInfo COM-based object model. These techniques are discussed in greater detail in Chapter 4, 'Programming ESRI applications'. The second line declares a variable that represents a rectangle with sides parallel to a coordinate system defining the extent of the data. You'll use pEnv to define the visible bounds of the map. The predefined variable, ThisDocument, is the IDocument interface to the MxDocument object that represents the ArcMap document. The ActiveView property provides an IActiveView interface that links the document data to the current screen display of that data. By reducing the size of the envelope that represents the extent of the map, the macro zooms in on the map's features once the screen display is refreshed.

4. Switch back to ArcMap.

5. In the Tools menu, select Macros and then Macros.

6. Select the NewMacros.MyZoomIn macro and click Run.

   The display zooms in.

Adding a macro to a toolbar

You'll want convenient access to the macros you write. You can add a macro to built-in toolbars or toolbars you've created.

1. In the Tools menu, select Customize.

2. In the Toolbars tab, create a new toolbar.

3. Switch to the Commands tab and select the Macros category.

4. In the Save in combo box, select the name of your project.

   The commands list at the right of the dialog lists NewMacros.MyZoomIn.

5. Drag the macro name to the toolbar you created.

   The macro appears with a default icon.

6. To change its properties, right-click the icon.

7. In the context menu that appears, select Change Button Image and choose a button from the palette of icons.

8. Close the Customize dialog.

9. Click the button to run the macro.

Invoking the Visual Basic Editor directly

As an alternative to the Create button in the Macros dialog, you can navigate directly to the Visual Basic Editor and create procedures on your own. In this section, you'll create a macro named MyZoomOut in the NewMacros module that will zoom out from the display. You can use the same code that you used for MyZoomIn, with only a minor modification to one line.

1. Press Alt+F11, the Visual Basic Editor's keyboard accelerator.

2. In the Visual Basic Editor's View menu, select Project Explorer.

3. In the Project Explorer, click the Project entry, then Modules, and then NewMacros.

4. In the Code Window, copy the MyZoomIn code from the beginning of the Sub to the End Sub.

5. Paste the MyZoomIn Sub code below the existing code.

6. Change the name of the copied Sub to MyZoomOut.

7. Change the line

   ```
   pEnv.Expand 0.5, 0.5, True
   ```

   to

   ```
   pEnv.Expand 1.5, 1.5, True
   ```

8. Follow steps 1–9 in the previous section of the tutorial, 'Adding a macro to a toolbar', to add and run your second macro.

Getting help in the Code Window

The two macros you've just completed perform operations similar to the Fixed Zoom In and Fixed Zoom Out commands on the Tools toolbar. You didn't really add any new functionality, but you've perhaps learned something about the object model and how to start to write some useful code. You can learn more about the methods with which you've worked by making use of the *ArcObjects Help* that's available in the Object Browser or in the Code Window.

1. In the Tools menu, select Macros and then Visual Basic Editor.

2. Locate the NewMacros module and in the My ZoomIn Sub click or double-click the method name Expand in the line

   ```
   pEnv.Expand 0.5, 0.5, True
   ```

3. Press the F1 key.

   The *ArcObjects Help* window displays the help topic for Expand.

In addition to *ArcObjects Help*, consult *ArcObjects Developer Help* in the ArcInfo program group for object model diagrams, samples, tips, and tricks.

Calling built-in commands

If you've read *Using ArcCatalog* or *Using ArcMap*, you know that the code you'll be writing will add functionality to what's already a rich environment. There may be instances in which you want to make use of several built-in commands executed in sequence or combine built-in commands with your own code. Calling existing commands involves working with the ArcID module. Using the Find method, the code locates the UID of the command in the ArcID module. If you want to look at the ArcID module in greater detail, it's in the Normal template of your application (either Normal.mxt or Normal.gxt).

To write a macro that calls existing commands, follow these steps. *Note that the Visual Basic line continuation character (an underscore) is used in this example and elsewhere in the tutorial due to space limitations of the book format only.*

1. In the Tools menu select Macros and then Visual Basic Editor.

2. In the NewMacros module create a Sub procedure with the following code:

```
Sub FullExtentPlus()
'
' macro: FullExtentPlus
'
    Dim intAns As Integer
    Dim pItem As ICommandItem
    With Project.ThisDocument.CommandBars
```

```
    Set pItem = _
    .Find(ArcID.PanZoom_FullExtent)
    pItem.Execute
    intAns = _
    MsgBox("Zoom to previous extent?", _
    vbYesNo)
    If intAns = vbYes Then
      Set pItem = _
    .Find(ArcID.PanZoom_ZoomToLastExtentBack)
      pItem.Execute
    End If
  End With
End Sub
```

3. Add the FullExtentPlus macro to a toolbar or menu.

4. Run the MyZoomIn macro and then run FullExtentPlus.

Creating a tool in VBA

To this point in the tutorial, you've only created commands. Commands, once invoked, usually perform some direct action without user intervention. As you've seen in the built-in toolbars and menus, users interact with other controls in addition to commands. As part of the customization environment, you can add sophisticated controls to toolbars and menus. These controls are called UIControls. You can read more about all the UIControls in Chapter 3, 'Customizing ESRI applications graphically'. In this section of the tutorial, you'll create a UIToolControl to interact with the ArcMap display.

1. In the Tools menu, select Customize.

2. In the Customize dialog box, select the Commands tab and then change the Save in combo box to the name of your project or Untitled.

3. In the Categories list, select UIControls.

4. Click New UIControl.

5. In the dialog that appears, choose UIToolControl as the UIControl Type and then click Create and Edit.

Adding code for the UIToolControl

The application adds an entry in the Object Box for a UIToolControl and stubs in an event procedure for the UIToolControl's Select event. You won't add any code to the Select event procedure at this time; instead, select the MouseDown event in the Events/Procedures box at the right-hand side of the Code Window. You'll add code to this event to enable you to drag a rectangle on the screen display; the application will zoom to the rectangle's extent.

1. Add the following code to the MouseDown event procedure.

```
If button = 1 Then
    Dim pDoc As IMxDocument
    Dim pScreenDisp As IScreenDisplay
    Dim pRubberEnv As IRubberBand
    Dim pEnv As IEnvelope
    Set pDoc = ThisDocument
    Set pScreenDisp = _
    pDoc.ActiveView.ScreenDisplay
    Set pRubberEnv = New RubberEnvelope
    Set pEnv = _
    pRubberEnv.TrackNew(pScreenDisp, Nothing)
    pDoc.ActiveView.Extent = pEnv
```

```
    pDoc.ActiveView.Refresh
End If
```

The key line of the procedure is the one containing the TrackNew method, which rubber-bands a new shape on the specified screen. The code uses the Envelope object that the method returns to set the new extent for the map.

When you selected the MouseDown event procedure to add code to it, you may have noticed that UIToolControl supports several other events. The Customization Framework handles many of the details of coding for you, so you only have to code the event procedures you need. Later in this tutorial, you'll find that this is in contrast to what is required when implementing a tool with an ICommand and an ITool interface as part of an ActiveX DLL.

A tool is not appropriate for all occasions. You can control when a UIToolControl is available by adding code to its Enabled event procedure.

2. Add the following code to the UIToolControl's Enabled event procedure.

```
Dim pDoc As IMxDocument
Set pDoc = ThisDocument
If pDoc.FocusMap.LayerCount > 0 Then
    UIToolControl1_Enabled = True
ElseIf pDoc.FocusMap.LayerCount = 0 Then
    UIToolControl1_Enabled = False
End If
```

3. Add the following code to the CursorID event procedure to control the cursor that appears when you use the tool.

```
UIToolControl1_CursorID = 3 'crosshair
```

4. To provide a ToolTip when the mouse hovers over the tool's button, add the following code to the ToolTip event procedure.

```
UIToolControl1_ToolTip = "Zoom to rectangle"
```

5. Add the following code to the Message event procedure to supply additional text describing the tool's functionality in the Status bar area.

```
UIToolControl1_Message = _
"Zooms to a designated rectangle"
```

6. In the Visual Basic Editor's File menu, select Close and Return to ArcMap.

7. In the Tools menu, select Customize and then choose the Commands tab.

8. Select the current document or Untitled in the Save in combobox.

9. In the Categories list, choose UIControls and then drag the UIToolControl you created to a toolbar and close the Customize dialog.

Try out the tool by selecting it and then dragging a rectangle on the display. You can also see the Enabled event procedure code in action if you remove all layers from the map. Once you add data back to the map, the tool will be enabled again.

Changing button properties

You can change the image on any toolbar button or menu command, except for a button that displays a list or a menu when you click it. You can display text, an icon, or both on a toolbar button. And you can display either an icon and text or text only on a menu command. You can change the image that represents the tool and other properties by right-clicking the button.

1. Right-click any toolbar and select Customize in the context menu that appears.

   Context menus are available throughout ArcMap and ArcCatalog. Click the right mouse button to determine whether a context menu is available.

2. Right-click the button whose properties you want to change.

3. In the context menu that appears, select Change Button Image and then choose an image.

   The image you chose appears on the face of the button.

4. Close the Customize dialog.

Creating a COM component

You can use the VBA environment embedded in ArcMap and ArcCatalog to accomplish most, if not all, of your personal or in-house customization and development tasks; however, your implementation tool preference, standard practice, or business plan may call for a development environment other than VBA, one that's external to ArcMap or ArcCatalog. Since the ESRI applications are COM clients—their architecture supports the use of software components that adhere to the COM specification—you can build components with different languages such as Visual Basic, Visual C++, Visual J++, and so on, and subsequently use them inside the applications.ESRI provides several COM-based object libraries, the same ones that are automatically referenced inside the VBA development environment, so you can get access to the appropriate functionality your development effort requires. COM concepts are discussed in greater detail in Chapter 4, 'Programming ESRI applications.' This section of the tutorial illustrates how to use Visual Basic, *not VBA*, to create a COM component, for use inside ArcMap. In this section of the tutorial you'll create a tool that lets you select the polygon features adjacent to a single polygon of a layer and displays a statistics dialog. The tutorial uses Microsoft Visual Basic 6.0.

Creating an ActiveX DLL project

Visual Basic lets you build several different kinds of projects. To create a component that works with ArcMap or ArcCatalog, you'll create an ActiveX DLL. An ActiveX DLL is a COM-enabled file that runs in the same memory space as the application that calls them. As such, they are referred to as in-process servers.

1. Start Visual Basic.

2. In the New Project dialog box, double-click the ActiveX DLL icon. Visual Basic automatically adds a class module, Class1, to the new project.

3. Press F4 to open the Properties window. Double-click the Name property and change it to AdjacentTool. This is the name you'll use to create objects from the class.

4. In the Project menu, click Project1 Properties to open the Project Properties dialog box. Select the General tab, change the Project Name to Tutorial, and then click OK.

5. In the File menu, select Save Project to save the project files. Name the class module Tutorial_AdjacentTool and name the project Tutorial. Visual Basic will provide the appropriate extensions.

Referencing the object libraries

To get access to the functionality you need, you must set a reference to the applicable object libraries. In this case, you'll set references to the ESRI Object Library and the ESRI ArcMap Object Library.

1. In the Project menu, select References.

2. In the References dialog, check ESRI ArcMap Object Library and then check ESRI Object Library.

   If these libraries don't appear in the References list, click Browse and locate esriMx.olb and esriCore.olb in the installation folder's help subfolder for example, D:\arcexe80\help.

3. Click OK.

Implementing the required interfaces

The class for AdjacentTool implements the ICommand and ITool interfaces. These interfaces are members of the ESRI Object Library (esriCore.olb). To create any type of command in Visual Basic for use with ArcInfo, you must implement ICommand. In addition, since you're creating a tool, you must also implement the ITool interface. Even if you don't need to write code for all the properties and methods of these interfaces to meet the requirements of your design, the class you create must be able to respond when any property or method of the interface is invoked. Therefore, every method and logical property in the interface must have an associated implementation in the class module. This requirement will be checked by Visual Basic's compiler. You cannot compile your code without supplying every implementation.

It's easy, though somewhat tedious, to create the procedure stubs for the method implementations if you use the keyword Implements at the top of the class module. The class module's editor window has a wizard bar that includes two dropdown combo boxes. If you select the name of the interface in the left-hand combo box, you can quickly generate the skeletons for the method implementations by selecting the method names in the right-hand combo box.

1. Add the following lines at the top of the AdjacentTool class module's code window.

    ```
    Option Explicit
    Implements ICommand
    Implements ITool
    Dim pApp as esriMx.Application 'ArcMap app
    Dim pDoc as IMxDocument
    ```

2. In the left-hand combo box select ICommand.

3. In the right-hand combo box select each method or logical property to create the stub code.

    Once you've selected a method or property it appears with a bold font.

4. Repeat steps 2 and 3 for ITool.

Adding code to distinguish the tool

Once you've created all the procedure stubs, you can add code to the procedures that distinguish the component in the application.

1. In the ICommand_Category procedure add the following line:

    ```
    ICommand_Category = "Tutorial"
    ```

    This code sets the name of the category to which the command belongs. The category appears in the list at the left-hand side of the Commands panel of the Customize dialog.

2. In the ICommand_Caption procedure add the following line:

    ```
    ICommand_Caption = "AdjacentTool"
    ```

    This is the string that will be used when the command is used as a menu item, and it also serves as the name of the command as it appears in the list at the right-hand side of the Commands panel of the Customize dialog when you click the Tutorial category.

3. In the ICommand_Name procedure add the following line:

    ```
    ICommand_Name = "Tutorial_AdjacentTool"
    ```

This code sets the internal name of the component. By convention it's the concatenation of the command's category and its caption.

Adding code to describe the tool

Next, you can add code to the procedures that describe the component or provide additional information.

1. In the ICommand_Message procedure add the following line:

```
ICommand_Message = "Selects features " & _
"adjacent to the feature you click on"
```

This code sets the message string that appears in the status bar area of the application when the mouse passes over the command.

2. In the ICommand_Tooltip procedure add the following line of code:

```
ICommand_Tooltip = "Select adjacent features"
```

This code sets the brief popup text that appears when the mouse hovers over the command.

If you want to provide more extensive information, you can add code to ICommand_HelpContextID and ICommand_HelpFile to specify the topic in the specified help file that contains information about the command. In this tutorial we'll just leave the stubs for these methods.

Adding code to set the tool's availability

The tool exists within an application and in an environment with other commands and tools. In order to make the tool easier to use and understand, you can make it available when appropriate conditions exist.

In order to set the context within which the code will run, you must establish a connection with the application. Recall that you made two declarations at the top of the class module. Here's where you'll make the initial assignment.

1. In the ICommand_OnCreate procedure add the following lines:

```
Set pApp = hook
Set pDoc = pApp.Document
```

The first line establishes a pointer to the application, using the method's hook argument. The second line retrieves a reference to the ArcMap document.

2. In the ICommand_Enabled procedure add the following code:

```
With pDoc.FocusMap
  If .LayerCount > 0 Then
    ICommand_Enabled = True
  ElseIf .LayerCount = 0 Then
    ICommand_Enabled = False
  End If
End With
```

This code enables the tool when there are one or more data layers on the map and disables it if there are no layers on the map.

3. In the ITool_Deactivate procedure add the following code:

```
ITool_Deactivate = True
```

This code deactivates the tool. If you were to leave this method uncoded, the default setting of False would prevent interaction with any other tool.

Adding code to set what the tool does

With the code that determines the characteristics of the tool in place, you can code what will happen when you use the tool. Since this particular tool uses the Query_SelectionStatistics command, you must export the ArcID module from ArcMap.

1. Start ArcMap and then press Alt+F11, the keyboard shortcut to display the Visual Basic Editor.

2. Press Ctrl+R, the keyboard shortcut to display the Project Explorer.

3. Double-click Normal and then double-click Modules.

4. Select ArcID.

5. In the File menu, select Export File.

6. In the dialog that appears, navigate to the folder containing Tutorial.vbp and then click Save.

7. Exit the Visual Basic Editor and exit ArcMap.

8. In Visual Basic, press Ctrl+D, the keyboard shortcut to add a file, navigate to the folder containing ArcID.bas, and then click Open.

9. Add the following code to the ITool_OnMouseDown procedure.

```
Dim pScreenDisp As IScreenDisplay
Dim pDt As IDisplayTransformation
Dim pPt As IPoint
Dim pMap As IMap
Dim pLayer As IFeatureLayer
Dim pSelEnv As ISelectionEnvironment
Dim pSelection As ISelection
Dim pEnumFeat As IEnumFeature
Dim pFeature As IFeature
Dim pFeatureCursor As IFeatureCursor
Dim pSpatialFilter As ISpatialFilter
Dim pFeatureSelection As IFeatureSelection
Dim pFillSymbol As ISimpleFillSymbol
Dim pColor As IRgbColor
Dim psym As ISymbol

Set pScreenDisp = _
pDoc.ActiveView.ScreenDisplay
Set pDt = pScreenDisp.DisplayTransformation
'get the MouseDown location in map units
Set pPt = pDt.ToMapPoint(X, Y)


'the tutorial expects the first layer to
'serve as the target
Set pMap = pDoc.ActiveView.FocusMap
Set pLayer = pMap.Layer(0)
pLayer.Selectable = True


'create a SpatialFilter to be used in
'a point in polygon selection
Set pSpatialFilter = New SpatialFilter
With pSpatialFilter
    Set .Geometry = pPt
    .GeometryField = _
    pLayer.FeatureClass.ShapeFieldName
    .SpatialRel = esriSpatialRelWithin
```

```
End With
Set pFeatureCursor = _
pLayer.Search(pSpatialFilter, False)
'pFeature is a polygon feature
Set pFeature = pFeatureCursor.NextFeature

'create a SpatialFilter to be used in the
'search for polygons adjacent to pFeature
Set pSpatialFilter = New SpatialFilter
With pSpatialFilter
   Set .Geometry = pFeature.Shape
   .GeometryField = _
   pLayer.FeatureClass.ShapeFieldName
   .SpatialRel = esriSpatialRelTouches
End With

Set pFeatureSelection = pLayer 'QI

pFeatureSelection.SelectFeatures _
pSpatialFilter, esriSelectionResultNew, False
pFeatureSelection.SetSelectionSymbol = True

Set pColor = New RgbColor
pColor.RGB = vbRed
Set pFillSymbol = New SimpleFillSymbol
pFillSymbol.Color = pColor
pFillSymbol.Style = esriSFSSolid

Set psym = pFillSymbol 'QI
Set pFeatureSelection.SelectionSymbol = psym
```

```
Dim pitem As ICommandItem
pDoc.ActiveView.Refresh

'finish by displaying
'statistics for the adjacent features
'ArcID is a VB module that was exported from
'ArcMap
Set pitem = pApp.Document.CommandBars _
.Find(ArcID.Query_SelectionStatistics)
pitem.Execute
```

Compiling the DLL

Once you've completed coding the tool, you must compile it to create the ActiveX DLL.

1. In the File menu, select Save Project.

2. In the File menu, select Make Tutorial.dll.

   At this point, it's good practice to switch your project's version compatibility option from Project Compatibility to Binary Compatibility.

3. In the Project menu, select Tutorial Properties and then click the Component tab.

4. Select the Binary Compatibility option and then click OK.

   Make sure the name of the DLL is displayed below the option; if it isn't, browse for it.

5. In the File menu, select Make Tutorial.dll to recompile the DLL.

Registering the COM component with ArcMap

Once you've created the ActiveX DLL, you'll want to use it in the application. To do this, you have to register the component with the application. ArcMap and ArcCatalog make this aspect of the process very simple.

1. Start ArcMap and in the Tools menu select Customize.
2. Click Add from file.
3. Navigate to the folder that contains Tutorial.dll.
4. Double-click the filename.

    The dialog that appears lists the components that will be registered with the application.

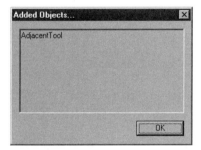

5. Click OK.

    The Categories list redraws. It now includes the Tutorial category.

Adding the component to the document

Now that the tool is registered with its client ArcMap, you can add it to a document or template.

1. In the Commands panel of the Customize dialog select the Tutorial category.

    The tool, AdjacentTool appears in the right-hand side Commands list.

2. In the Save in combo box, select the name of the document, Normal.txt, or Untitled.
3. Drag AdjacentTool to a toolbar.
4. Right-click AdjacentTool; in the context menu that appears, select Image and Text.
5. Right-click AdjacentTool again; in the context menu that appears, select Change Button Image to choose a bitmap.
6. Click Close.
7. Select the AdjacentTool, then click a polygon feature.

    The tool selects the adjacent features and displays the Selection Statistics dialog.

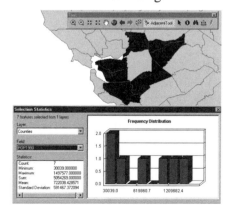

What's next?

Now that you've completed the tutorial, review what you've done and decide what you want to do next.

In the first section of the tutorial you learned how to change the way ArcCatalog and ArcMap look by customizing these applications graphically. You worked with menus, tools, and toolbars. You became familiar with the Customize dialog and saved your work in a template.

In the second section of the tutorial you used the development environment that's embedded in the ESRI applications, Visual Basic for Applications (VBA), to create your own commands or macros.

In the third section of the tutorial you took a closer look at the ESRI Object Library and created an ActiveX DLL in Visual Basic that served as a COM component for ArcMap.

At this point, you can continue to read this book sequentially or chart your own course. Chapter 3 provides you with a detailed look at how to customize the applications graphically. If you prefer, however, skip to Chapter 4 to learn more about programming the ESRI applications. The first part of Chapter 4 describes the concepts and techniques of working with the ESRI object model and in the process, provides a basic introduction to the key concepts in COM. The rest of the chapter contains some basic information about the VBA development environment that's embedded in the applications and some special considerations if you work with Visual Basic. Once you've completed Chapter 4, you may choose to read more detailed descriptions about specific areas of the object model in Chapters 5 through 8. Here's where you can study code examples that may match your interests— they might even provide you with ideas or impetus for further work. If you want to learn more about working with CASE tools, follow the tutorial that's in Chapter 9. Finally, if you're considering packaging your work in an extension, you'll find Chapter 10 of interest.

If you learn best by studying or trying out code, another source of additional examples is the online help system. If you're looking for examples of how to use Visual C++ with the ESRI Object Library, you'll find them in the *ArcObjects Developer Help* file. You can display this file from the ArcInfo program group in the Start menu. In addition, *ArcObjects Help* (esricore.hlp), the reference file for the ESRI object library, is available in the Object Browser and in the Code Window in Visual Basic development environments. The file itself is located in the <installation directory>\help folder.

Whatever your specific objectives may be, we hope that this book proves useful along the way to achieving them.

Customizing ESRI applications graphically

3

Although ESRI end-user applications are designed to be flexible and easy to use, you may want the ArcMap and ArcCatalog interfaces to reflect your own preferences and the way you work. If you work in a larger organization, others may want you to develop a customized work environment for them. As a developer, you'll be glad to learn that many of the customization tasks you may be asked to perform can be handled without writing a single line of code; in fact, you may be able to instruct others on how to use the customization environment themselves to create the look and feel they want on their own. You can change or create toolbars, menus, keystrokes, and so on, to help you get your work done in the most efficient way. Not only can you change the way the existing work environment is organized, but you'll also be able to provide additional functionality by linking code you or others have written to menu commands or tools. This chapter shows that the customization environment for ESRI applications is rich with possibilities.

Basic user interface elements

ESRI applications all have Main Menu and Standard toolbars, which appear by default. Both are referred to as *toolbars*, although the Main Menu toolbar contains menus only. Toolbars can contain menus, buttons, tools, combo boxes, or edit boxes, which are different types of commands. Whether it's built into the application or it's something you've created yourself, code is associated with each command. All commands execute in generally the same manner, although you use each type differently when interacting with the application. These are the types you'll work with:

- *Menus* arrange other commands into a list. A *context menu* is a floating menu that pops up at the location of the pointer when you press the right mouse button.

- *Buttons* and *menu items* run a script when you click them.

- *Tools* require interaction with the display before an action is performed—that is, before their script is run. The Zoom In tool is a good example of a tool—you click or drag a rectangle over a map before seeing its contents in more detail.

- *Combo boxes* let you choose an option from a dropdown list. For example, in ArcMap you can choose the layer(s) from which you want to select features when working with a map.

- *Text boxes* or *Edit boxes* let you type in text. In ArcMap you can type the scale at which you want to view the map.

The tasks in this book apply to all types of commands unless otherwise noted. The task's description will note any exceptions that apply for specific types of commands.

Docking toolbars

Any toolbar can be *docked* at the top or bottom or to the left or right side of the ArcMap or ArcCatalog windows. Alternatively, toolbars can float on the desktop while functioning as part of the application. When you dock a toolbar, it is moved and resized

with the application's window. To prevent a toolbar from docking, hold down the Ctrl key while dragging it.

The Catalog tree in ArcCatalog and the table of contents in ArcMap are docked on the left by default, but you can dock them elsewhere in the window, or you can position them so they float on the desktop as well.

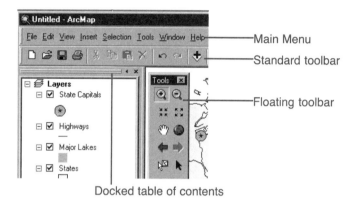

Docked table of contents

Changing the way the application looks

Whether you want to position toolbars in a specific area of the application, group commands in a way that works best for you, add new macros or load add-ins that you've gotten from another source, load styles, or always work with the same geographic data, you'll find that you can customize ESRI applications in numerous ways. One of the principle ways in which to tailor the applications to suit your needs is to use the Customize dialog box to change menus and toolbars. You can carry out many of the tasks described in the rest of this chapter by starting with this dialog box. Select Customize in the Tools menu or right-click any open toolbar and choose Customize from the toolbar's shortcut menu. The Customize dialog box resembles and has many of the same properties as the equivalent dialog in the Microsoft Office 97 applications. If you've used any of these applications, the environment will be familiar to you.

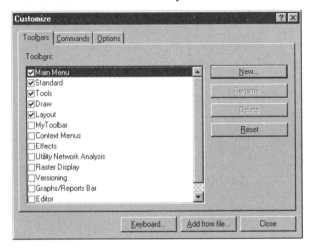

The Toolbars tab of the Customize dialog box

When you open the Customize dialog box, you can modify existing menus, toolbars, and context menus with simple drag-and-drop techniques. You can create your own menus, toolbars, and context menus, too. Don't worry; if you change things radically and would prefer to return the user interface to its built-in settings, you can do so easily. For more information see "Resetting a built-in toolbar" later in this chapter.

Where to save your changes

ArcMap comes with a Normal template (the Normal.mxt file), which opens and places the toolbars and the ArcMap table of contents in their built-in positions. If you want to make changes that appear every time you open ArcMap, save them in the Normal template. In ArcMap, you work with a map document (an .mxd file). You might want to make changes that only appear when working with a particular map. For example, you might want your custom query and analysis toolbar to appear only in specific maps. By default, all of your changes are saved in the Normal template; however, once you make a change and save it in the current document, all subsequent changes will be saved in the current document by default.

Suppose you've created more than just a custom toolbar—you've created an entire environment with custom tools and macros that are used only when you edit a dataset's features. You can save this environment as a customized template. When you create a new map document, you can choose to base it on the Normal template or your custom template. By convention, ArcMap templates have the extension .mxt. For more information on saving customized templates, see 'Saving customizations in a template' later in this chapter.

Hiding and showing toolbars

In addition to the Main Menu and the Standard toolbars, ESRI applications have other toolbars that contain commands to help you perform a group of related tasks. ArcMap has buttons on the Standard toolbar for quickly displaying its most commonly used toolbars. Both ArcCatalog and ArcMap let you hide or show toolbars from the Toolbars list in the View menu or the Customize dialog box. A check mark next to the toolbar name indicates that it's visible. However, although it appears in the list, you can't hide the Main Menu. After checking a toolbar, the application displays it as a floating toolbar on the desktop. If the toolbar was previously turned on, it returns to its last position.

Tip

Shortcut to the Toolbars list

You can access the Toolbars list without using the View menu. Simply right-click any toolbar, the status bar, or the title bar of the table of contents in ArcMap or the Catalog tree in ArcCatalog.

Tip

Hiding floating toolbars
To quickly hide a floating toolbar, click its Close button.

Hiding and showing toolbars from the View menu

1. Click View and point to Toolbars.

2. Check a toolbar to show it.

   Uncheck a toolbar to hide it.

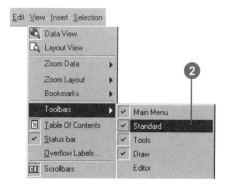

Toggling toolbars from the Customize dialog

1. Click the Tools menu and click Customize.

2. Click the Toolbars tab.

3. Check a toolbar to show it.

   Uncheck a toolbar to hide it.

4. Click Close.

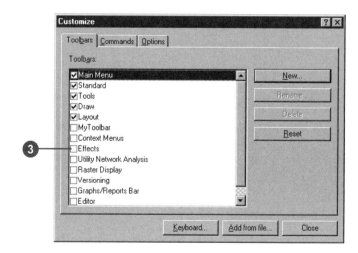

Creating custom toolbars

Several toolbars are provided with ArcMap and ArcCatalog, but you may want to create a new toolbar with buttons to run your custom scripts. You can rename and delete custom toolbars, but you can't rename or delete the toolbars that are built into the applications.

Tip

Renaming toolbars

You can rename a toolbar created in ArcMap or ArcCatalog with the New button of the Customize Dialog; on the other hand, if the toolbar is part of an ActiveX DLL that you added with the Add from file button, it cannot be renamed.

Creating a new toolbar

1. Click the Tools menu and click Customize.

2. Click the Toolbars tab.

3. Click New.

4. Type in the name of your new toolbar.

5. Click the dropdown arrow of the Save in combo box and choose the template in which this toolbar will be saved.

6. Click OK.

   The new, empty toolbar appears in the Toolbars list and is displayed in the application as a floating toolbar.

7. Click Close.

Renaming a toolbar

1. Click the Tools menu and click Customize.

2. Click the Toolbars tab.

3. Click the toolbar you want to rename.

4. Click Rename.

5. Type the name of your toolbar.

6. Click OK.

   The renamed toolbar appears in the application as a floating toolbar in the application.

7. Click Close.

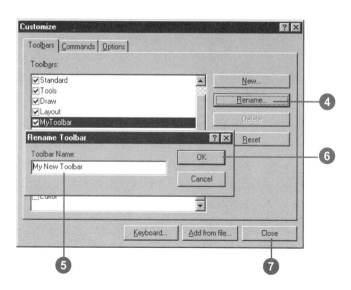

Deleting a toolbar

1. Click the Tools menu and click Customize.

2. Click the Toolbars tab.

3. Click the custom toolbar that you want to delete.

4. Click Delete.

5. Click Close.

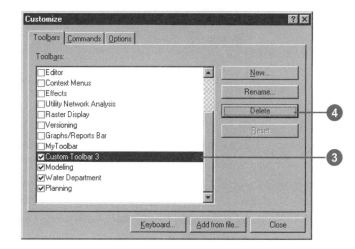

Adding a new, empty menu to a toolbar

1. Show the toolbar to which you want to add a new, empty menu.

2. Click the Tools menu and click Customize.

3. Click the Commands tab.

4. Click New Menu in the Categories list.

5. Click and drag the New Menu command from the Commands list and drop it on the toolbar.

   An empty menu called "New Menu" appears in the toolbar.

6. Right-click New Menu in the toolbar.

7. Type an appropriate caption for the menu in the text box.

8. Press Enter.

9. Click Close.

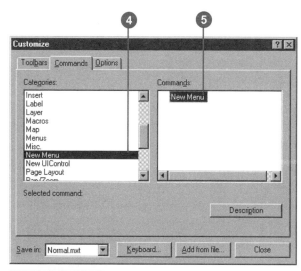

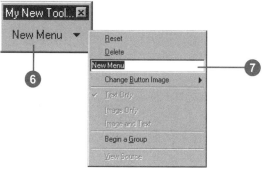

Modifying context menus

ArcMap and ArcCatalog contain several context menus to provide easy access to commands appropriate to the task at hand. By clicking the right-mouse you'll see the built-in context menus. You can add a command to any of the listed context menus should your work require it.

Adding a built-in command to a context menu

1. Click Tools and then click Customize.

2. Click the Toolbars tab.

3. Check the Context Menus toolbar.

4. Click Context Menus on the Context Menus toolbar.

   A list of all the context menus in the application appears.

5. Click the arrow for the context menu to which you want to add a command.

   The context menu's commands are listed.

6. Click the Commands tab in the Customize dialog box.

7. Click the category that contains the command you want to add to the menu.

8. Click and drag the command from the Commands list and drop it on the context menu.

   The command appears in the context menu.

9. Click Close in the Customize dialog box.

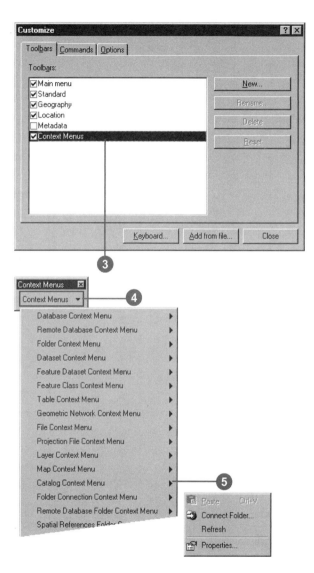

Changing a toolbar's contents

You can modify the contents of any toolbar by adding, moving, and removing commands. Grouping commands together on a toolbar can help to visually separate commands used for different tasks such as browsing and querying. After modifying a built-in toolbar, you can return it to its original contents; you might want to do this if you accidentally remove a command from the toolbar.

Tip

About the Save in combo box

The Save in combo box appears on the Commands tab, in the New toolbar dialog, in the Reset toolbar dialog, and in the Customize Keyboard dialog. Use this setting to specify whether the change you are about to make will be saved in Normal or in another template.

Adding a command

1. Click the Tools menu and click Customize.

2. Click the Toolbars tab.

3. Make sure the toolbar you want to change is checked.

4. Click the Commands tab.

5. In the Save in combo box, click the dropdown arrow and choose the template in which the changes to the toolbar will be saved.

6. Click the category that contains the command you want to add.

7. Click the command you want to add.

8. Drag the command you want to add to any location on the target toolbar.

9. Repeat steps 6 through 8 until all the commands you want are added.

10. Click Close.

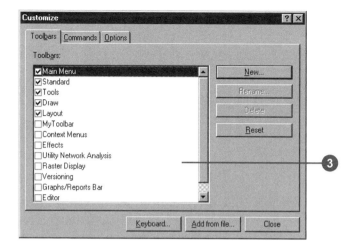

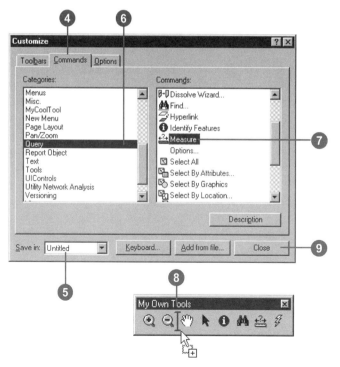

Moving a command

1. Show the toolbar with the command you want to move.

2. If you're moving the command to another toolbar, show the destination toolbar.

3. Click the Tools menu and click Customize.

4. Drag the command to its new position and then drop it.

   The command appears in the new position.

5. Click Close in the Customize dialog.

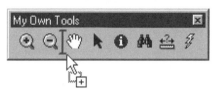

Tip

Removing commands

When you remove a command from a toolbar, you're not deleting it; it's merely no longer available on the toolbar. If you decide to, you can always add a command back to the same toolbar or to a different one.

Removing a command

1. Show the toolbar containing the command that you want to remove.

2. Click the Tools menu and click Customize.

3. Drag the tool you want to remove from the toolbar.

   The mouse pointer changes to a line through a circle.

4. Drop the command.

5. Click Close in the Customize dialog box.

Grouping commands

1. Show the toolbar containing the commands that you want to group together.

2. Click the Tools menu and click Customize.

3. Right-click the command located to the right of where the grouping bar should be placed.

4. Check Begin a Group.

   A grouping bar appears in the toolbar.

5. Click Close in the Customize dialog.

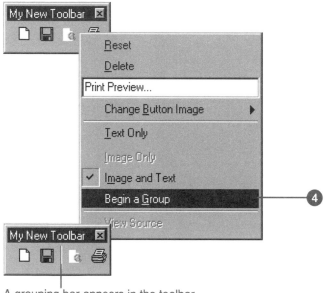

A grouping bar appears in the toolbar.

Resetting a built-in toolbar

1. Click the Tools menu and click Customize.

2. Click the Toolbars tab.

3. Click the built-in toolbar that you want to reset.

4. Click Reset.

5. Click the dropdown arrow and choose the template in which the changes to the toolbar settings were made.

6. Click OK.

7. Click Close.

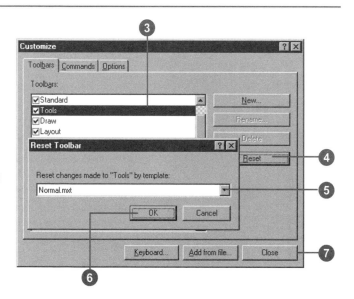

Changing a command's appearance

You can modify the display type, caption, and image of a menu, button, or tool without programming. By default, a button or tool dropped directly onto a toolbar has the display type Image Only, while it has the display type Image and Text when dropped onto a menu. Menus can only have the display type Text Only. The caption is the text that appears with the appropriate display types. Menus and their contents can be accessed from the keyboard by holding down Alt and then pressing the underlined letter. Create one of these access keys by typing an ampersand (&) in front of a letter in the caption.

Other command properties can only be modified with programming—such as ToolTip and Message. When you hold the mouse pointer over a command, its ToolTip displays as a short message in a floating yellow box. A command's Message displays in the status bar.

Changing the display type

1. Show the toolbar containing the command whose display type you want to change.

2. Click the Tools menu and click Customize.

3. In the toolbar, right-click the command you want to change.

4. Check Image Only to display only the command's image.

   Check Text Only to display only the command's caption.

   Check Image and Text to display both its image and its caption.

5. Click Close in the Customize dialog box.

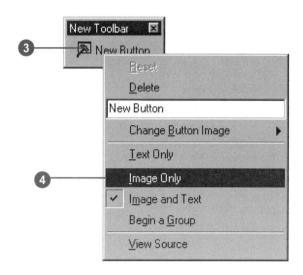

Changing the caption

1. Show the toolbar containing the command whose caption you want to change.

2. Click the Tools menu and click Customize.

3. In the toolbar, right-click the command you want to change.

4. Type a new caption in the text box on the context menu.

5. Press Return.

6. Click Close in the Customize dialog box.

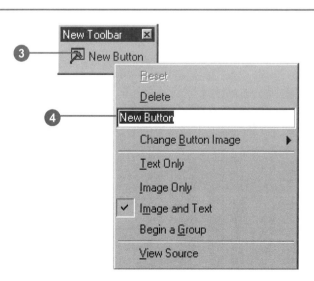

See Also

To learn how to set the properties of commands in code, see Chapter 2, 'Quick-start tutorial', and Chapter 5, 'Working with the Customization Framework'.

Changing the image

1. Show the toolbar containing the command whose image you want to change.

2. Click the Tools menu and click Customize.

3. In the toolbar, right-click the command you want to change.

4. Point to Change Button Image.

5. Click one of the images displayed. Or click Browse, navigate to a custom image, and then click Open.

   The new image appears if the command has the appropriate display type.

6. Click Close in the Customize dialog box.

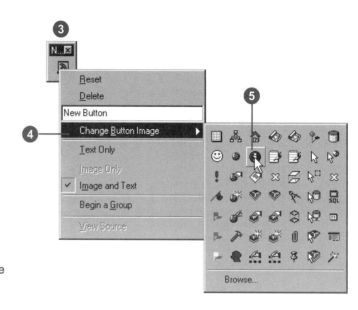

Resetting a built-in command

1. Show the toolbar with the command you want to reset.

2. Click the Tools menu and click Customize.

3. In the toolbar, right-click the command you want to change.

4. Click Reset.

   The command returns to its built-in settings.

5. Click Close in the Customize dialog.

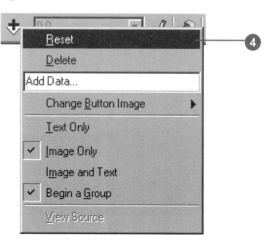

Creating shortcut keys

When you access a menu from the keyboard using its access key, the menu opens and you can see its contents. In contrast, a command's shortcut key executes the command directly without having to open and navigate the menu first. For example, Ctrl+C is a well-known shortcut for copying something in Windows. One command can have many shortcuts assigned to it, but each shortcut can only be assigned to one command. A command's first shortcut is displayed to its right if the command appears in a menu.

Assigning a shortcut key

1. Click the Tools menu and click Customize.

2. Click Keyboard.

3. Click the category containing the command you want to modify.

4. Click the command to which you want to add a keyboard shortcut.

5. Click in the shortcut key text box and then press the keys on the keyboard that you want to use for a shortcut.

   If those keys have been assigned to another command, that command's name will appear below.

6. Click the dropdown arrow and choose the template in which the shortcut key will be saved.

7. Click Assign if the keys aren't currently assigned to another command.

   The new shortcut appears in the Current Key/s list.

8. Click Close in the Customize Keyboard dialog box.

9. Click Close in the Customize dialog box.

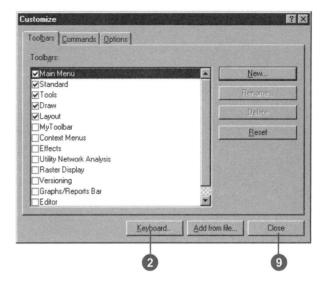

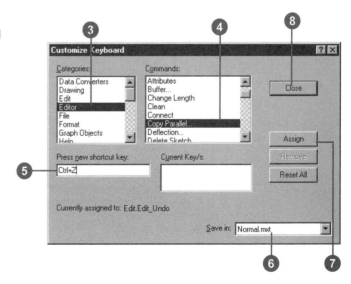

Removing a keyboard shortcut

1. Click the Tools menu and click Customize.

2. Click Keyboard.

3. Click the category that contains the command you want to modify.

4. Click the command from which you want to remove a keyboard shortcut.

5. Click the dropdown arrow in the Save in combo box and choose the template from which to delete the shortcut key setting.

6. Click the shortcut in the Current Key/s list that you want to delete.

7. Click Remove.

8. Click Close in the Customize Keyboard dialog box.

9. Click Close in the Customize dialog box.

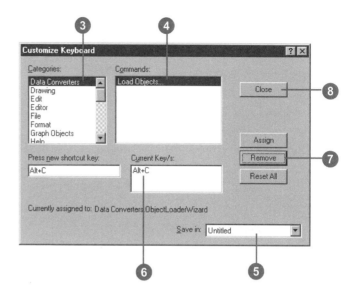

Resetting built-in keyboard shortcuts

1. Click the Tools menu and click Customize.

2. Click Keyboard.

3. Click the dropdown arrow in the Save in combo box and choose the template whose shortcut keys will be reset.

4. Click Reset All.

5. Click Close in the Customize Keyboard dialog box.

6. Click Close in the Customize dialog box.

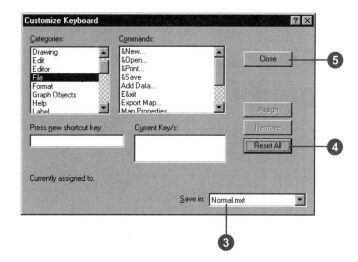

Saving customizations in a template

If you create a map that contains customizations or code you'd like to use as the basis for other maps, or if you modify an existing template and want to use it again, you can save it as a template. The template will contain all customizations that were made graphically as well as any modules created in the Visual Basic Editor.

You can save a map template anywhere on your network. When you want to use the template, you can open it from ArcMap.

If you save a template in the ArcMap Templates folder (the <installation directory> \bin\Templates folder), it will show up in the list of templates on the New map document dialog box. You can also create subfolders in this folder, and they'll show up as separate tabs on this dialog—when you click each tab you'll see the templates in that folder.

Saving a template

1. Click File and click Save As.

2. Click the dropdown arrow and click ArcMap Templates.

3. Navigate to the folder where you want the template saved.

4. Type a name for the new template.

5. Click Save.

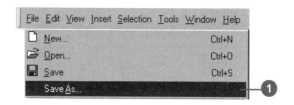

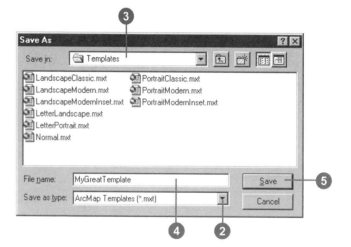

Saving a template so it will appear in a new tab

1. Click File and click Save As.

2. Click the dropdown arrow and click ArcMap Templates. ▶

3. Navigate to the Templates folder.

4. Click the New Folder button.

5. Type the name of the new folder—this name will appear on the New map document dialog as a tab.

6. Double-click the new folder.

7. Type the name of the new template.

8. Click Save.

   The next time you start a map from a template, you'll see a new tab with your template on the New map dialog box.

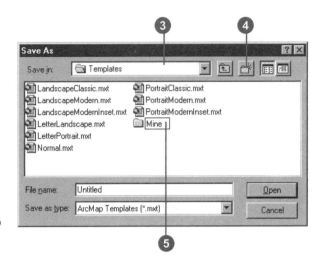

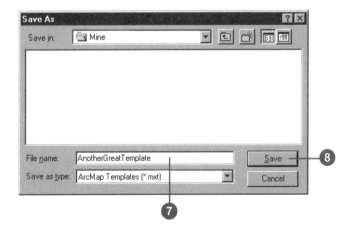

Setting toolbar options

The Options tab in the Customize dialog box lets you specify the size of icons on buttons and whether ToolTips will appear on all the toolbars in ArcMap or ArcCatalog when you let the mouse hover over a button.

Later this chapter shows how the Options tab also provides a means to lock or unlock the Customize dialog, the Macros dialog, and the Visual Basic Editor. In addition, you can use the Options tab to change VBA security and update the status of the Normal template's ArcID module.

Displaying toolbars with large icons

1. Click the Tools menu and click Customize.

2. Click the Options tab.

3. Check Large icons to display large icons for a toolbar's buttons.

4. Click Close.

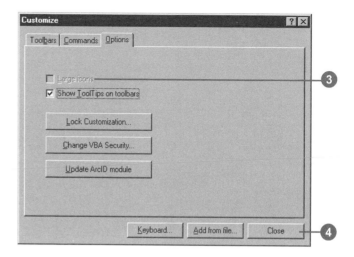

Showing ToolTips on toolbars

1. Click the Tools menu and click Customize.

2. Click the Options tab.

3. Check Show ToolTips on toolbars to display ToolTips for the buttons on a toolbar.

4. Click Close.

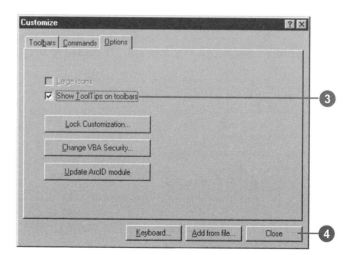

Creating, editing, and running macros

Both ArcCatalog and ArcMap come with Visual Basic for Applications. VBA is not a standalone program. It provides an integrated programming environment that lets you write a Visual Basic (VB) macro and then debug and test it right away in Catalog or Map. You can run macros by choosing Macros from the Tools menu, or you can add them to a toolbar as a button. You can write macros that integrate some or all of VB's functionality with the extensive object library that Map and Catalog expose. The object library is always available to you in the VBA environment.

You can save the code you write in the Visual Basic Editor (VBE) in the map document or in a specific template as part of a module—simply open the appropriate document in the Project window. A code window appears for the document; in the window, you create a macro by creating a VB Sub procedure. You can open more than one code window at the same time; this lets you easily copy and paste code between these windows or even import code stored in external files.

Creating a macro in the Visual Basic Editor

1. Click the Tools menu, point to Macros, then click Macros.

2. Type the name of the macro you want to create In the Macro name text box.

3. Press the Enter key or click Create.

   The stub for a Sub procedure for the macro appears in the Code window.

   If you don't specify a module name, the application stores the macro in a module named NewMacros.

4. Type the code for the macro.

5. Click the VBE File menu and click Save Project.

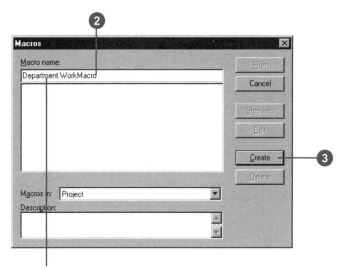

Preceding the name of a macro with a module's name and a dot stores it in the specified module.

Editing a macro in the Visual Basic Editor

1. Click the Tools menu, point to Macros, then click Macros.

2. In the list below the Macro name text box, select the name of the macro you want to edit.

3. Click Edit.

   The code that's been written for the macro appears in the Code window.

4. Edit the code.

5. Click the VBE File menu and click Save Project.

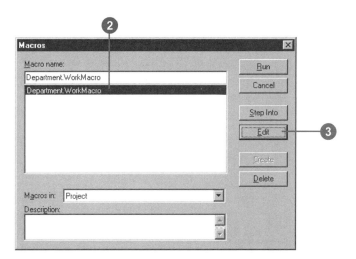

Running a macro from a Visual Basic module

1. Open the template or document that contains the macro.

2. Click the Tools menu, point to Macros, and then click Macros.

3. Type the name of the macro you want to run in the Macro name text box.

4. Click Edit.

5. Click Run Sub/UserForm.

Running a macro in the Macros dialog box

1. Open the document or template that contains the macro.

2. Click the Tools menu, point to Macros, and then click Macros.

3. Type the name of the macro you want to run in the Macro name text box.

4. Click Run.

Adding a macro to a toolbar

1. Show the Destination toolbar.

2. Click the Tools menu and click Customize.

3. Click the Commands tab.

4. Click Macros in the Categories list.

5. Click and drag the macro from the Commands list and drop it on the toolbar.

6. Click Close.

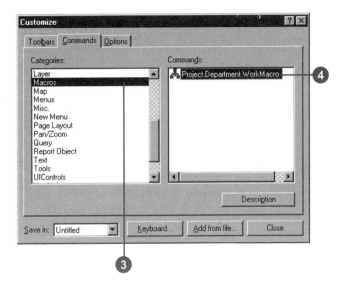

Creating custom commands with VBA

Applications such as ArcMap and ArcCatalog use Automation (formerly OLE Automation)—a feature of the industry-standard technology called the Component Object Model (COM)—to expose their objects to development tools, macro languages, and other applications that support Automation. For example, ArcMap exposes a Map, a PageLayout, a LineFillSymbol, and so on, each as a different type of object. ArcCatalog exposes different objects germane to its functionality.

When an application supports Automation, the objects the application exposes can be accessed by VB. You can use VB to manipulate these objects by invoking methods on the object or by getting and setting the object's properties. Each object must satisfy a specific set of requirements.

Toolbars and commands are COM objects, too. To be a command, the object must meet a basic set of requirements for all commands; to be a button, the object must also satisfy the button requirements. Many of the user interface aspects of ►

Creating a new command

1. Show the toolbar to which you want to add a new command.

2. Click the Tools menu and click Customize.

3. Click the Commands tab.

   If you're working with ArcMap, specify the document in which to save your work in the Save in dropdown list.

4. Click UIControls in the Categories list.

5. Click New UIControl.

6. Click the type of UIControl you want to create.

7. Click Create to create the control without attaching code to it.

   The name of the control appears in the commands list. You can add code for the control at another time. If you want to start adding code to the control right away, click Create and Edit and skip to step 10. ►

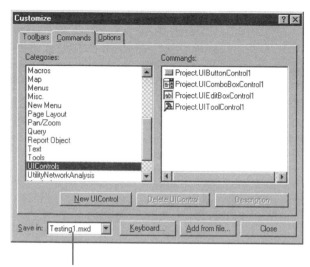

If you're working with ArcMap, specify the document in which to save your work in the Save in combo box.

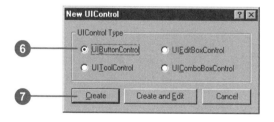

commands and toolbars have been handled for you as part of the customization environment. You can then attach behavior that incorporates aspects of the applications' extensive object models.

Subsequent chapters and the online Help describe the interfaces, methods, coclasses, and enumerations that may be used in the development environment that's built into your ESRI applications.

There is an easy way to create custom commands with VBA. You create a new button, tool, combo box, or edit box (collectively called UIControls); attach code to the control's events, such as what happens when you click a button; and then drag an instance of the control onto a toolbar. To allow you to reuse the controls and the code associated with them, you can save them in the Normal template or another template or document.

8. Click and drag the newly created UIControl and drop it on a toolbar or menu.

Once it's on the toolbar or menu, right-click the button to set its image, caption, and other properties.

9. Right-click the new control and then click View Source.

The Visual Basic Editor appears, displaying the control's code in the code window.

10. Click one of the control's event procedures.

11. Type code for the event procedure.

12. Repeat steps 10 and 11 until all the appropriate event procedures have been coded.

13. Click Save in the Visual Basic Editor.

14. Click the Close button in the Visual Basic Editor.

15. If you clicked Create and Edit in step 7, open the Customize dialog box, click the Commands tab, and drag the newly created UIControl from the commands list to a toolbar or menu.

16. Click Close in the Customize dialog box.

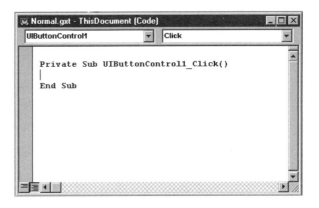

Working with UIControls

UIControls provide a way to enrich an application in addition to button clicks and menu selections. The event procedures associated with these controls allow you to respond to user interaction and update controls based on the state of the application. Because UIControls can appear in menus or on toolbars, they may let you avoid having to display a dialog box or UserForm.

The *UIButtonControl* works similarly to the built-in buttons that come with the application. Typically, you use a UIButtonControl to start, end, or interrupt an action or series of actions. You can write code to set whether it appears enabled or appears as if it is pressed in. You can also set its ToolTip, provide a message that will appear in the status bar, and respond to its Click event.

The *UIToolControl* works similarly to the built-in tools that come with the application. Typically, you use a UIToolControl to perform some type of interaction with the display. You can write code to toggle whether the tool appears as enabled or set its ToolTip. You can respond to mouse and key events. In addition, you can have it respond when the user selects the tool, double-clicks it, or right-clicks it. You can write for the UIToolControl when the map refreshes or when the tool is deactivated.

The *UIComboBoxControl* works similarly to the combo boxes that appear as part of the interface. It combines the features of a text box and a list box. Typically, you use a UIComboBoxControl to provide a set of choices from which a

selection can be made. You can also type into the edit box portion of the control. The combo box has methods that allow you to populate its list or remove individual or all items. Several properties associated with the combo box let you work with items, return the index of the selected item, return the text at a specific index, return the text in the control's edit box, and determine how many items are in the control. In addition, you can respond to several events including when the user makes a change in the edit portion of the control or when a change to the selection occurs. As with the UIButtonControl, you can set the control's ToolTip and provide a status bar message.

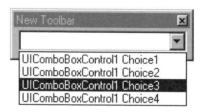

The *UIEditBoxControl* works similarly to the edit boxes that appear as part of the interface. Typically, you use a UIEditBoxControl to display information entered by the user. The control can also display data derived from an external source. You can use its Clear method to remove its contents, and its Text property contains the text that's displayed. You can specify whether the control appears as enabled. In addition, you can respond to when the user makes a change or presses a key. As with the UIButtonControl, you can set this control's ToolTip and provide a status bar message.

Adding custom commands

You don't have to use VBA to create custom commands—in fact, in some cases your custom commands may require you to use another development environment. You can create custom objects in any programming language that supports COM; see the subsequent chapters in this book for details. Custom commands or toolbars created outside VBA are often distributed as ActiveX DLLs. After adding a custom object into ArcMap or ArcCatalog, you can use it as you would any built-in command.

Tip

Register the ActiveX DLL

Prior to adding a custom command from a file, make sure that either you or the installation process by which you acquired it, registers its ActiveX DLL.

1. Click the Tools menu and click Customize.

2. Click Add from file.

3. Navigate to the file containing the custom command.

4. Click the file and click Open.

   The Added Objects dialog box appears, reporting which new objects have been registered on your computer.

5. Click OK.

6. Click the Toolbars tab.

7. Check the toolbar to which you want to add the custom command.

8. Click the Commands tab.

9. Click the custom command's category in the Categories list.

10. Click and drag the command from the Commands list and drop it on the toolbar.

11. Click Close.

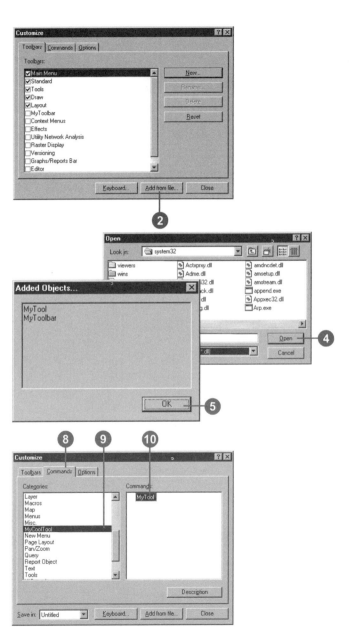

Updating the ArcID module

If you are developing applications or writing macros that make use of COM objects that you've added in, you can update the Normal.ArcID module to include newly added commands. In this way, you'll be able to refer to the COM objects you've added in by name when using a method such as CommandBars.Find. Updating also allows you to keep Normal.ArcID up to date should you remove a command.

See Also

For more information about the Normal template's ArcID module see Chapter 5, 'Working with the Customization Framework'.

1. Click the Tools menu and click Customize.

2. Click the Options tab.

3. Click Update ArcID Module.

4. Click Close.

   When you use the ArcID module in code that you write, commands that you've added will appear with the other identifiers in Visual Basic's code completion feature. You can specify to auto list members as you type in the Editor tab of the Options dialog.

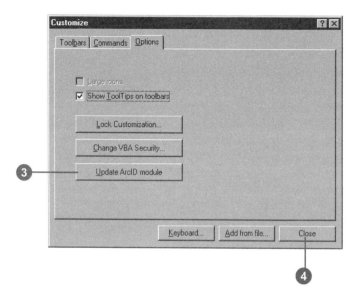

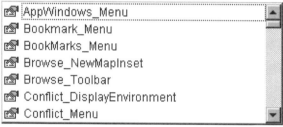

VB's code completion feature lists ArcID members in response to the Find method.

Locking customization, documents, and templates

In order to protect proprietary or sensitive information or work in progress or to prevent others from changing the way you've customized a document or template, you can use the Lock Customization facilities provided in the Options tab of the Customize dialog box. In addition, Lock Customization prevents access to the Macros dialog box and the Visual Basic Editor. For locking individual documents or templates while still allowing access to the Visual Basic Editor, you can use the Protection tab of the VBA Project Properties dialog box. This dialog lets you password protect the ArcMap document or template you've saved.

See Also

You can create your own customization filter to control what aspects of the customization environment other users will have access to. For an example written in VBA, see Chapter 5, 'Working with the Customization Framework'.

Locking Customization

1. Click the Tools menu and click Customize.

2. Click the Options tab.

3. Click Lock Customization.

4. In the dialog that appears, enter a password that has at least five alphanumeric characters and then confirm it.

   To use the Customize dialog, the Macros dialog, or the Visual Basic Editor with the document or template subsequently, the correct password must be supplied.

5. Click OK in the Lock Customization dialog.

6. Click Close.

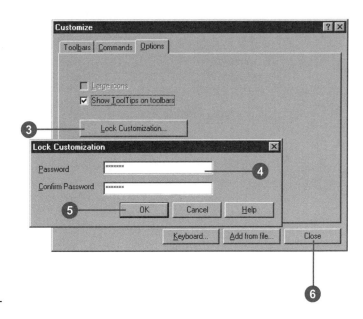

Unlocking Customization

1. Click Tools, then click Customize or choose Macros, then click Macros or Visual Basic Editor.

   The Unlock Customization dialog appears.

2. Enter the password to unlock your selection.

3. Click OK.

   The Customize dialog appears. If you specify an incorrect password, a message appears.

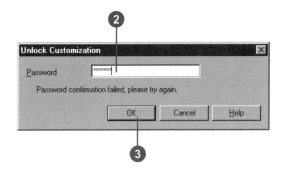

See Also

For more information about templates, see Chapter 5, 'Working with the Customization Framework'.

Tip

Change your mind?

If you haven't yet dismissed the Customize dialog after specifying a password, you can change or remove the password by clicking Unlock Customization on the Options tab dialog.

Locking documents and templates

1. Click the Tools menu, point to Macros, and then click Visual Basic Editor.

2. In the Project Explorer, right-click the project or template you want to lock and then click Project Properties.

3. Click the Protection tab.

4. Check Lock project for viewing to lock the project so that it cannot be viewed or edited.

5. Type a password and confirm it.

6. Click OK in the Project Properties dialog box.

7. Click Save Project.

   The next time someone opens the Project and attempts to view the Project Properties, they'll be prompted for a password.

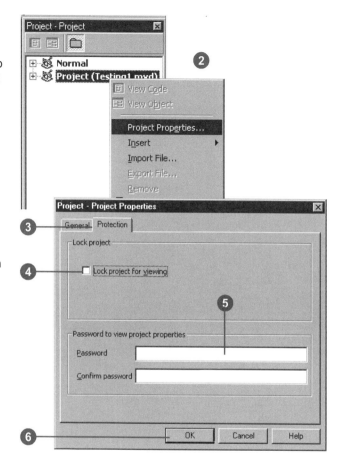

Changing VBA Security

A macro virus is a type of computer virus that's stored in a macro within a document, template, or add-in. When you open such a document or perform an action that triggers a macro virus, the macro virus might be activated, transmitted to your computer, and stored in your Normal template. From that point on, every document you open could be automatically "infected" with the macro virus; if others open these infected documents, the macro virus is transmitted to their computers.

ESRI applications offer the levels of security described in the Security dialog box to reduce the chances of macro viruses infecting your documents, templates, or add-ins.

See Also

To learn more about using digital signatures and about how security levels and digital signatures work together, see Chapter 5, 'Working with the Customization Framework'.

1. Click the Tools menu and click Customize.

2. Click the Options tab.

3. Click Change VBA Security.

4. Click the level of security you want.

5. Click the Trusted Sources tab to see a list of the names of organizations or individuals whose signed macros will be allowed to run.

   When you check the Always trust macros from this source check box in the Security Warning dialog box, which appears when you open a document or template with macros, this digital certificate is added to the Visual Basic for Applications Trusted Sources list.

6. Click OK.

7. Click Close.

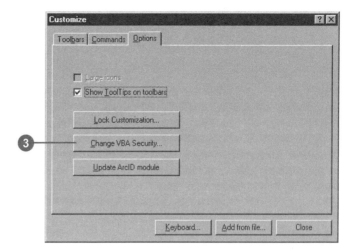

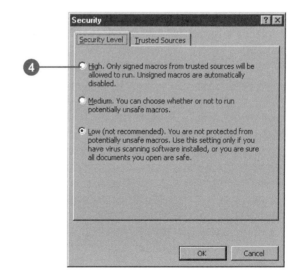

Programming ESRI applications

4

Chapter 2 presented a tutorial to get started quickly, and Chapter 3 discussed how to customize ESRI applications graphically. This chapter discusses the rudiments of the development environment embedded within ArcInfo 8 and shows how you can work with an external development environment (Visual Basic) to provide additional functionality. Once you've gained some familiarity with Visual Basic and COM, you may want to move to the discussions of the various parts of the object model in Chapters 5 through 8. If you're new to the Visual Basic development environment or want to learn the fundamentals of programming ESRI applications, this chapter's for you.

COM and ArcInfo

If you followed the tutorial in Chapter 2, you received a quick introduction to working with VBA, Visual Basic, and the ArcInfo COM-based object model—however, we left the whys and wherefores for later. Let's take a look now at the technology on which ArcInfo is based and see what implications it has for the way you carry out your programming tasks.

COM technology

The ArcInfo applications, ArcMap and ArcCatalog, are based on the technology called COM. COM is a protocol that connects one software component, or module, with another. By making use of this protocol it's possible to build reusable software components that can be dynamically interchanged in a distributed system.

To "get" COM (and therefore all COM-based technologies), it's important to realize that it isn't an object-oriented language, but a protocol or standard. COM doesn't specify how an application should be structured. As an application programmer working with COM, language, structure, and implementation details are left up to you. COM does specify an object model and programming requirements that enable COM objects (also called COM components, or sometimes simply *objects*) to interact with other objects. These objects can be within a single process, in other processes, or even on remote machines. They can and have been written in other languages and may have been developed in very different ways. That is why COM is referred to as a binary specification or standard—it is a standard that applies after a program has been translated to binary machine code.

COM allows these components to be reused at a binary level, meaning that third party developers do not require access to source code, header files, or object libraries in order to extend the system even at the lowest level.

Clients and servers

Within COM there is the notion of clients and servers. The server provides some functionality, and the client uses that functionality. As stated earlier, COM facilitates the communication between these two types of components. An individual component can act as both a client and a server.

The client and its servers can exist in the same process or in a different process space. In-process servers are packaged in Dynamic Link Library (DLL) form, and these DLLs are loaded into the client's address space when the client first accesses the server. When you created the COM component in the Chapter 2 tutorial, you created an ActiveX DLL, an in-process server. Out-of-process servers are packaged in executables (EXE) and run in their own address space. There are pros and cons to each method of packaging that are symmetrically opposite. DLLs are faster to load into memory, and calling a DLL function is faster. Executables, on the other hand, provide a more robust solution (if the server fails, the client will not crash), and security is better handled since the server has its own security context. In a distributed system EXEs are more flexible, and it does not matter if the server has a different byte ordering than the client.

In a COM system the client, or user of functionality, is isolated completely from the provider of that functionality, the server. All that the client needs to know is that the functionality is available; with that knowledge, the client can make calls to the server and expect the server to honor them. In this way COM is said to act as a contract between client and server. If the server breaks that contract, the behavior of the system will be unspecified. In this way COM development is based on trust between the implementer and the user of functionality. In the ArcInfo applications there are many servers that provide, via their interfaces, thousands of properties and methods. When you use the ESRI object libraries you can assume that all these properties and interfaces have been fully implemented, and if they are present on the object diagrams, they are there to use.

COM classes

Developing with COM means developing using interfaces. All communication between COM components is made via the components' interfaces.

COM interfaces are abstract, meaning there is no implementation associated with an interface; the code associated with an interface comes from a class implementation. The interface sets out what requests can be made of an object that chooses to implement the interface. How that interface is implemented can be different between objects. Thus the objects inherit the type of interface, not its implementation, which is called *type inheritance*. You model functionality abstractly with the interfaces.

COM classes provide the code associated with one or more interfaces, thus encapsulating the functionality entirely within the class. Two classes can both have the same interface, but they may implement them quite differently. By implementing these interfaces in this way, COM displays classic object-oriented polymorphic behavior. COM does not support the concept of multiple inheritance; however, this is not a shortcoming since individual classes can implement multiple interfaces.

In the detailed object model diagrams that are included with the *ArcObjects Developer Help* file, you'll see three types of classes: Abstract classes, CoClasses, and Classes.

An Abstract class cannot be created but is solely a specification for instances of subclasses (through type inheritance). Dataset or Geometry classes are examples of these abstract objects.

An object that is a CoClass can be created explicitly. CoClasses are instantiable as well as creatable. Instantiable means that an instance of this class can be created; creatable means that you

can explicitly create them in VB using New. Fields, Field, and Point objects fall into this category.

An object that is a Class can not be created, but objects of this class can be created as a property of another class or instantiated by objects from another class. Clients (especially Visual Basic applications) cannot create these objects explicitly, but they can be instantiated by calling certain ArcInfo 8 methods. An example of these objects is a FeatureCursor. You cannot create a FeatureCursor object using New, but a FeatureCursor object is created internally by the system when you call the Search method on IFeatureClass.

Interfaces

COM interfaces are how COM objects communicate with each other. When working with COM objects the developer never works with the COM object directly but gains access to the object via one of its interfaces. COM interfaces are designed to be a grouping of logically related functions. The virtual functions are called by the client and implemented by the server.

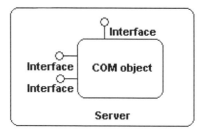

A COM object's services are accessed through its interfaces.

The IUnknown interface

All COM interfaces derive from the IUnknown interface, and all COM objects must implement this interface. The IUnknown interface performs two tasks: it controls object lifetime and provides run-time type support. It is through the IUnknown interface that clients maintain a reference on an object while it is in use—leaving the actual lifetime management to the object itself. Clients also use IUnknown to acquire other interfaces on an object. To perform these functions IUnknown has three methods. *QueryInterface* is the method that a client calls when another interface on the object is required. You'll often hear or see it referred to as 'QI'. When a client calls QueryInterface the object provides an interface and calls *AddRef*. In fact, it is the responsibility of any COM method that returns an interface to increment the reference count for the object on behalf of the caller. The client must call the *Release* method when the interface is no longer needed. AddRef is called explicitly by the client only when an interface is duplicated.

It's good practice in Visual Basic to call Release explicitly by assigning an interface equal to *Nothing* to release any resources it's holding. Note that even if you don't call Release, Visual Basic will automatically call it when you no longer need the object—that is, when it goes out of scope. In Visual Basic the system performs all these reference counting operations for you, making the use of COM servers relatively straightforward. In C++, however, you must increment and decrement the reference count to allow an object to correctly control its own lifetime. Likewise, the QueryInterface method must be called when asking for another interface. In C++ the use of smart pointers simplifies much of this. These smart pointers are class based and hence have appropriate constructors, destructors, and overloaded operators to automate much of the reference counting and query interface operations.

Inbound and outbound interfaces

Interfaces can be either inbound or outbound. An inbound interface is the most common kind—the client makes calls to functions within the interface contained in the server. An outbound interface is one where the server makes calls to the client—a technique analogous to the traditional callback mechanism. There are differences in the way these interfaces are implemented. The implementer of an inbound interface must implement all functions of the interface; failure to do so breaks the contract of COM. You saw how to do this in Visual Basic in the Chapter 2 tutorial when you generated the skeletons for the method implementations of ICommand and ITool. When the developer of the client implements an outbound interface, not all functions present on the interface must be implemented. This is only the case in Visual Basic since it provides stub methods behind the scenes; however, in C++ you must implement all the pure virtual functions to compile the class. To handle the outbound interface IActiveViewEvents in Visual Basic that is the default outbound interface of the Map class, you must use the WithEvents keyword and then provide appropriate functions to handle the events.

```
Private WithEvents pMapEvents as Map
Private Sub pMapEvents_SelectionChanged()
    ' User changed feature selection
    ' update my feature list form
    UpdateMyFeatureForm
End Sub
```

Default interfaces

Every COM object has a default interface that is returned when the object is created if no other interface is specified. All the objects within the ESRI object libraries have IUnknown as their default interface, with a few exceptions; for example, the default interface of the Application object for both ArcCatalog and ArcMap is set to the IApplication interface.

With some implementations of COM a class may choose to implement the IDispatch interface. The object classes within the ESRI object libraries do not implement the IDispatch interface; for this reason, the object libraries cannot be used with late-binding scripting languages like JavaScript™ or VBScript, since these languages require that all COM servers accessed support the IDispatch interface. Careful examination of the ArcInfo Class Diagrams does indicate some interfaces where IDispatch is used. This is because there is a requirement in VBA for the IDispatch interface.

When an interface has been published it is not possible to change the external signature of that interface. It is possible at any time to change the implementation details of an object that exposes an interface. This change may be a minor bug fix or a complete reworking of the underlying algorithm; the clients of the interface do not care since to them the interface appears the same. This means that when upgrades to the servers are deployed in the form of new DLLs and EXEs, existing clients need not be recompiled to make use of the new functionality. If the external signature of the interface is no longer sufficient, a new interface is created to expose the new functions.

Invoking QueryInterface in Visual Basic code

Assuming an object supports two interfaces. You've got a reference to the first interface, and you called a method on it. To call a second method on the second interface you use QueryInterface. In other words, you need to query the second interface from the first to access the second method. The Point object in ArcInfo 8 supports another interface ITopologicalOperator, which contains methods like Buffer. Here is how you can invoke QI in Visual Basic:

```
Dim pPt As IPoint
Set pPt = New Point
pPt.PutCoords 100, 100
Dim pTopoOptr As ITopologicalOperator
Dim pBufferGeo As IPolygon
Set pTopoOptr = pPt ' QI for ITopologicalOperator
                        ' from IPoint
Set pBufferGeo = pTopoOptr.Buffer(20)
```

Note that a reference to an interface is also a reference to the object that implements the interface. In the code above, pPt or pTopoOptr are references to IPoint and ITopologicalOperator interfaces, respectively, but they are not objects themselves; rather, they are two object references pointing to the same Point object underneath.

When you assign a Point object to a variable of type ITopologicalOperator (as in Set pTopoOptr = pPt), Visual Basic asks the Point object if it supports the ITopologicalOperator interface by doing a QI. If the answer is yes, the object is assigned to that variable. Otherwise, a "Type mismatch" error will be raised:

Interface inheritance

An interface consists of a group of methods and/or properties. If one interface is designated to inherit from another, then all of the methods and/or properties in the parent are directly available in the inheriting object. Note that the underlying principle here is *interface inheritance,* rather than *implementation inheritance* that you may have seen in SmallTalk or C++. In implementation inheritance, an object inherits actual code from its parent; whereas in interface inheritance, it's the definition of the methods of the object that is passed on. COM uses the principles of containment or aggregation to achieve the actual code reuse. In your work, you'll see that Visual Basic's IntelliSense handles the interface inheritance by supplying the inherited methods and/or properties during code completion. An example of interface inheritance is the relationship between IFeature and IRow. IFeature inherits from IRow. This means that the Value property in IRow is directly available in IFeature. Thus if you have a variable pFeat of type IFeature you can directly call pFeat.Value. Without interface inheritance between IFeature and IRow, it would be necessary for you to QI for IRow interface on the Feature object first.

```
Dim pRow as IRow
Dim pFeat as IFeature
Set pFeat = SomeFunction() ' returns IFeature
Set pRow = pFeat
Debug.Print pRow.Value
```

Instead you can write the above code as:

```
Dim pFeat as IFeature
Set pFeat = SomeFunction() ' returns IFeature
Debug.Print pFeat.Value
```

Interface inheritance is shown in the ArcInfo 8 object model diagrams using a colon (:) between the two interfaces, for example, `IFeature:IRow`. This bit of information can prove quite valuable but is not available in the Object Browser, so make sure to consult the diagrams; for example, most geometry interfaces inherit from IGeometry.

Extensibility

As you've seen in the Chapter 2 tutorial and in *ArcObjects Developer Help,* you can extend a COM client such as ArcMap or ArcCatalog by creating new COM servers that serve up new or improved functionality. These new servers can be created from scratch, or they can use COM containment or COM aggregation to reuse existing functionality. For a third party developer to make use of existing components using either containment or aggregation, the only requirement is that the component that is being contained or aggregated is installed on both the developer and target client machines.

The simplest form of binary reuse is *containment.* With containment, the contained object (inner) has no knowledge that it is contained within another object (outer). The outer object must implement all the interfaces supported by the inner. When requests are made on these interfaces, the outer object simply delegates them to the inner. To support new functionality the outer object can either implement one of the interfaces without passing the calls on or implement an entirely new interface in addition to those interfaces from the inner object.

COM *aggregation* involves an outer object that controls which interfaces it chooses to expose from an inner object. The inner object is aware that it is being aggregated into another object and forwards any QueryInterface calls to the outer (controlling) object so that the object as a whole obeys the laws of COM. To the clients of an object using aggregation, there is no way to distinguish which interfaces are implemented by the outer object and which are implemented by the inner.

Component categories are used by client applications to efficiently find all components of a particular type that are installed on the system. For example, a client application may support a data export function in which you can specify the output format—a component category could be used to find all the data export components for the various formats. If component categories were not used, the application would have to instantiate each COM component and interrogate it to see if it supported the required functionality, which is not a practical approach. Component categories support the extensibility of COM by allowing the developer of the client application to create and work with classes that belong to a particular category. If at a later date a new class is added to the category, the client application need not be changed to take advantage of the new class, it will automatically pick up the new class the next time the category is read. See Chapter 10, 'Building and delivering extensions', for more information about working with component categories.

COM makes use of the Windows system registry to store information about the various parts that compose a COM system. The classes, interfaces, DLLs, EXEs, Type Libraries, and so forth, are all given unique identifiers, which the COM run-time system uses when referencing these components. These identifiers are commonly referred to as GUIDs (globally unique identifiers). To see an example of this, run regedit, open HKEY_CLASSES_ROOT, and search for esriCore entries in the CLSID key.

GUIDs, IIDs, CLSIDs, and ProgIDs

COM interfaces and coclasses are identified by a GUID. The GUID for an interface is called an interface ID (IID). The GUID for a coclass is called a class ID (CLSID). A ProgID is a text alias for a CLSID; the ProgID is a string composed of the project name and the class name of the coclass.

The ESRI Object Library's UID coclass can be used to represent the GUID of an object.

In the following VB example, u is defined as a new UID object and is set to the CLSID of the ArcMap AddData command. Now u can be used in any of the methods that require a UID object.

```
Dim u As New UID
u.Value = "{E1F29C6B-4E6B-11D2-AE2C-080009EC732A}"
```

In the following example, u is set to the ProgID of the ESRI Object Editor extension.

```
Dim u As New UID
u = "esriCore.Editor"
```

There is a built-in module called ArcID in the VBA project for the Normal template in both ArcMap and ArcCatalog. This module is a utility for finding the UID of the built-in commands and toolbars. You pass the name of a command or toolbar in as an argument to ArcID, and the UID of that item is returned. The ArcID module is regenerated every time the Normal template is loaded; the registry is read to get the GUIDs of all the commands and toolbars that the application currently uses.

Coding techniques for ArcInfo

Keeping the COM principles of the previous section in mind, we'll take a look now at how to carry out the key techniques that you'll make use of as you work with the ESRI object libraries.

Introducing the ESRI object libraries

If you use the VBA development environment embedded in ArcMap or ArcCatalog to write your code, you'll discover that it automatically includes a reference to the ESRI object library as well as the ArcMap object library or the ArcCatalog object library. Developing in an environment outside ArcMap or ArcCatalog, for example, Visual Basic, requires loading the object libraries by hand.

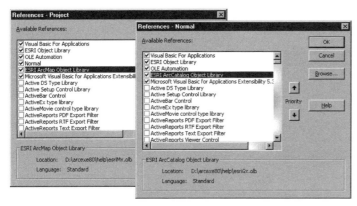

References to the ESRI object libraries are set automatically in ArcMap and ArcCatalog.

These object libraries are files that contain descriptions of the interfaces, coclasses, properties, methods, events, and enumerations that ArcMap or ArcCatalog expose. No matter what development environment you use, declaring object variables as a qualified class of an object—known as early binding—

increases the speed of your code because the development environment can detect the ESRI application objects at design time rather than at run time. A tangible advantage of setting object references this way is VBA's IntelliSense code completion feature. When you compile code during design time, VBA checks for programming errors and correct syntax and matches object types against object libraries. If you use a general variable type, such as Object—known as late binding—VBA doesn't interpret it until run time. This extra querying step decreases the speed of your program.

To see IntelliSense code completion in action, declare a variable as part of the esriCore library and then add a period after the library name. In this case, you'll see a list of the object types you can declare. You can use this popup box to quickly choose an ESRI application object type. To do this, scroll through the list until you find the appropriate entry and press SPACEBAR to enter it in your code.

Here is an example of code completion:

```
Dim pVar As esriCore.
```

Viewing Automation descriptions

You can view the ArcMap or ArcCatalog Automation descriptions and copy code templates using the Object Browser. The Object Browser displays the classes, properties, methods, events, and constants available from object libraries and the procedures in your project. You can use it to find and use objects you create as well as objects from other applications.

To display the Object Browser, choose Object Browser from the View menu. To browse or search the ArcMap or ArcCatalog objects, properties, methods, events, and constants, type the name of the object, property, method, event, or constant you want to search for in the Search Text text box or just click any member in the Members Of list.

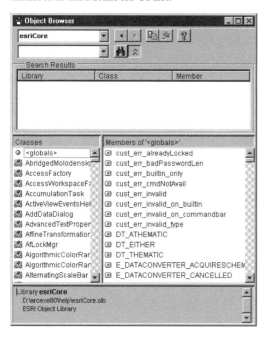

To restrict the list in the Object Browser to objects solely in the ESRI object library, choose *esriCore* in the Project/Library combo box at the top of the dialog. To restrict the list to the ArcMap object library, choose *esriMx,* and to restrict the list to the ArcCatalog object library, select *esriGx.*

The Object Browser is a convenient mechanism for viewing the ESRI object library; however, it has some inherent limitations. The default interface for most of the objects in the ESRI object library is IUnknown. Because the methods on the IUnknown interface are not callable in Visual Basic, the Object Browser does not show any properties or methods for ESRI Object Library coclasses in the Members of list. This limitation extends to the Locals window, which doesn't list the properties of local variables that are set to objects that have IUnknown as their default interface (even though you may have declared these variables as a particular interface).

Copying code templates

The Object Browser displays ArcMap or ArcCatalog properties, methods, events, and constants as members in the Members Of list. The Details pane at the bottom of the dialog displays the syntax for the members as a code template that you can copy and paste or select and then drag and drop into a module and substitute the appropriate variables and arguments.

Using ArcInfo 8 objects

To use an ArcInfo 8 object in Visual Basic or VBA, you must first get a reference to an interface that the object supports. Then you can call any method belonging to the interface. Let's say you want to initialize a point with an x,y value pair; you can invoke the PutCoords method on IPoint, an interface that Point object supports.

```
Dim pPt As IPoint
Set pPt = New Point
pPt.PutCoords 100, 100
```

The first line of this simple code fragment illustrates how to declare a variable for holding a reference to the interface that the object supports. The line reads the IID for the IPoint interface from the ESRI object library. You may find it less ambiguous, particularly if you reference other object libraries in the same project to precede the interface name with the library name, for example:

```
Dim pPt As esriCore.IPoint
```

That way, if there happens to be another IPoint referenced in your project, there won't be any ambiguity as to which one you are referring to.

The second line of the fragment creates an instance of the object or coclass (**c**omponent **o**bject **class**), and it assigns the default interface to pPt, which, you will recall, is IUnknown. Again with a name for the coclass as common as Point, you may want to precede the coclass name with the library name, for example:

```
Set pPt = New esriCore.Point
```

The last line of the code fragment invokes the PutCoords method. If a method can't be located in the vtable due to an error of some sort, you'll see the following error message in Visual Basic:

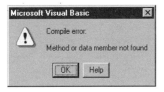

Using the ThisDocument object

Each VBA project has a ThisDocument module. Unlike other ArcInfo 8 objects, you don't have to set a reference to ThisDocument. If you want to manipulate the document associated with your VBA project or get its properties, simply use ThisDocument, for example:

```
Dim pDoc As IMxDocument
Set pDoc = ThisDocument
MsgBox pDoc.FocusMap.Layer(0).Name
```

Working with properties

Some properties refer to specific objects in the ESRI object library and other properties have values that are standard data types such as strings, numeric expressions, Boolean values, and so forth. For object references, declare an object variable and use the Set statement to assign the object reference to the property. For other values, declare a variable with an explicit data type or use Visual Basic's Variant data type. Then use a simple assignment statement to assign the value to the variable.

As you might expect, some properties are read-only, others are write-only, and still others are read/write. See the esriCore Help file for details about properties including what their read/write status is.

Working with methods

Methods perform some action and may or may not return a value. In some instances, a method returns a value that's an object, for example, in the code fragment below, EditSelection returns an enumerated feature interface:

```
Dim pApp As IApplication

Dim pEditor As IEditor

Dim pEnumFeat As IEnumFeature 'Holds the
selection

Dim pID As New UID

'Get a handle to the Editor extension

pID = "esriCore.Editor"

Set pApp = Application

Set pEditor = pApp.FindExtensionByCLSID(pID)

'Get the selection

Set pEnumFeat = pEditor.EditSelection
```

In other instances a method returns a Boolean value reflecting the success of an operation or writes data to a parameter; for example, the DoModalOpen method of GxDialog returns a value of True if a selection occurs and writes the selection to an IEnumGxObject parameter.

Working with events

Events let you know when something has occurred. You can add code to respond to an event. For example, a UIButtonControl has a Click event. You add code to perform some action when the user clicks the control. You can also add events that certain objects generate. VBA and Visual Basic let you declare a variable with the keyword WithEvents. WithEvents tells the development environment that the object variable will be used to respond to the object's events. The declaration must be made in a class module or a form. Here's how you'd declare a variable "with events" in the Declarations section:

```
Dim WithEvents p_viewEvents as Map
```

Once you've declared the variable, search for its name in the Object combo box at the top left of the Code window. Then inspect the list of events you can attach code to in the Procedure/ Events combo box at the top right of the Code window:

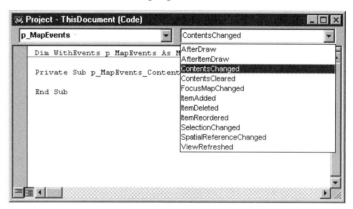

Objects as parameters

Some ArcInfo 8 methods expect objects for some of their parameters. In some cases you'll have to create the object first; in others the method will return one for you. As a general rule of thumb, the method name will be your guide. For example, if you have a polygon (pPolygon) whose center point you want to get, you can write code like this:

```
Dim pArea As IArea

Dim pPt As IPoint

Set pArea = pPolygon ' QI for IArea on pPolygon

Set pPt = pArea.Center
```

Note that you don't need to create pPt because the Center method creates a Point object for you.

Let's say you have the same polygon, and you want to get its bounding box. To do this, you use the QueryEnvelope method on IPolygon. If you write the following code:

```
Dim pEnv As IEnvelope
pPolygon.QueryEnvelope pEnv
```

you'll get an error because the QueryEnvelope method expects you (the client) to create the Envelope. The method will modify the envelope you pass in and return the changed one back to you.

How do you know when to create and when not to create? In general, all methods that begin with "Query" expect you to create the object such as QueryEnvelope. If the method name were GetEnvelope, then an object would be created for you.

When you write code to pass an object reference from one form, class, or module to another, for example:

```
Public Sub DoPoint(pPt As IPoint)
    <Code here>
End Sub
```

Your code passes a pointer to an instance of the Point class. This means that you are only passing the reference to the object, not the object itself; if you add the ByVal keyword as follows:

```
Public Sub DoPoint(ByVal pPt As IPoint)
    <Code here>
End Sub
```

This does not pass the object by value. Rather, it passes the interface by value. So the interface is copied, not the object. This means that the routine can make changes to the object but not to the object reference.

Using the TypeOf keyword

To check whether an object supports an interface (before you actually acquire a new interface), you can use Visual Basic's TypeOf keyword. For example, given an item selected in

ArcMap's Table of Contents, you can test whether it is a FeatureLayer, as in the following code:

```
Dim pDoc As IMxDocument
Dim pUnk As IUnknown
Dim pFeatLyr As IFeatureLayer
Set pDoc = ThisDocument
Set pUnk = pDoc.SelectedItem
If TypeOf pUnk Is IFeatureLayer Then      ' can we
QI for IFeatureLayer?
    Set pFeatLyr = pUnk      ' actually QI happens
here
    ... ' Do something with pFeatLyr
End If
```

Using the Is operator

If your code requires you to compare two object reference variables, you can use the Is operator. Typically, you can use the Is operator in the following circumstances:

- To check if you've got a valid object

```
Dim pPt As IPoint
Set pPt = New Point
If Not pPt Is Nothing Then 'a valid pointer?
... ' do something with pPt
End If
```

- To check if two object variables are referring to the same actual object.

Let's say you've got two object variables of type IPoint: pPt1 and pPt2. Are they pointing to the same object? If they are, then pPt1 Is pPt2.

- To find out if a certain method on an object returns a copy of or a reference to the real object.

In the following example, the Extent property on a map (IMap) returns a copy, while the ActiveView property on a document (IMxDocument) always returns a reference to the real object.

```
Dim pDoc As IMxDocument
Dim pEnv1 As IEnvelope, pEnv2 as IEnvelope
Dim pActView1 As IActiveView
Dim pActView2 as IActiveView
Set pDoc = ThisDocument
Set pEnv1 = pDoc.ActiveView.Extent
Set pEnv2 = pDoc.ActiveView.Extent
Set pActView1 = pDoc.ActiveView
Set pActView2 = pDoc.ActiveView
' Extent returns a copy,
' so pEnv1 Is pEnv2 returns False
Debug.Print pEnv1 Is pEnv2
' ActiveView returns a reference,
' so pActView1 Is pActView2
Debug.Print pActView1 Is pActView2
```

Iterating through a collection

In your work with ArcMap and ArcCatalog, you'll discover that in many cases you'll be working with collections. You can iterate through these collections with an *enumerator*. An enumerator is an interface that provides methods for traversing a list of elements. Enumerator interfaces typically begin with IEnum and have two methods, Next and Reset. Next returns the next element in the set, and Reset resets the enumeration sequence to the beginning.

Here is some VBA code that loops through the selected features (IEnumFeature) in a map. To try the code, add the States sample layer to the map and use the Select tool to select multiple features (drag a rectangle to do this). Add the code to a VBA macro and then execute the macro. The name of each selected state will be printed in the debug window.

```
Dim pDoc As IMxDocument
Dim pMap As IMap
Dim pEnumFeat As IEnumFeature
Dim pFeat As IFeature
Set pDoc = ThisDocument
Set pMap = pDoc.FocusMap
Set pEnumFeat = pMap.FeatureSelection
Set pFeat = pEnumFeat.Next
Do While Not pFeat Is Nothing
    Debug.Print _
    pFeat.Value(pFeat.Fields _
    .FindField("state_name"))
    Set pFeat = pEnumFeat.Next
Loop
```

Working with VBA

This section of the chapter discusses how to program in the VBA environment to control either ArcMap or ArcCatalog by accessing the objects they expose. Your code manipulates the objects by getting and setting their properties, such as setting the MaximumScale and MinimumScale of a Map's FeatureLayer; invoking methods on the objects, such as adding a vertex to a polyline; or setting a field's value. The code runs when an event occurs, for example, when a user opens a document, clicks a button, or alters data by modifying an EditSketch.

First, though, we'll look at the aspects of the VBA development environment in which you'll do your work that are specific to the ESRI applications. Consult Visual Basic Reference, the online help file that displays when you click Microsoft Visual Basic Help in the Help menu for generic help on the user interface, conceptual topics, how-to topics, language reference topics, customizing the Visual Basic Editor, and user forms and controls.

The VBA development environment

In the VBA development environment you can add modules, class modules, and user forms to the default project contained in every ArcMap or ArcCatalog document. A project can consist of as many modules, class modules, and user forms as your work requires. A *project* is a collection of items to which you add code. A *module* is a set of declarations followed by procedures—a list of instructions that your code performs. A *class module* is a special type of module that contains the definition of a class including its property and method definitions. A *user form* is a container for user interface controls such as command buttons and text boxes.

ArcMap has a default project associated with its document that's listed in the Project Explorer as Project followed by its filename. In addition, you'll see another project listed in the Project Explorer called Normal (Normal.mxt).

Normal is, in fact, a template for all documents. It's always loaded into the document. It contains all the user interface elements that users see as well as the class module named ArcID, which contains all the UIDs for the application's commands.

Since any modifications made to Normal will be reflected every time users create or open a document, needless to say you should be careful when making changes to Normal.

In ArcMap users can start by opening a template other than the default template. These templates are available to them in the New dialog. From a developer's perspective this is a base template, a document that loads an additional project into the document; it is listed in the Project Explorer as the TemplateProject followed by its filename. This project can store code in modules, class modules, or forms, and any other customizations such as maps with data, page layout frames, and so on. Any modifications or changes made to this base template are reflected only in documents that are derived from it.

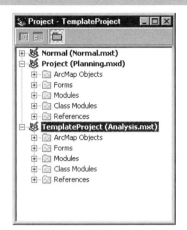

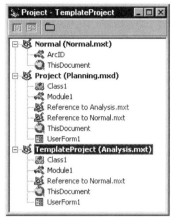

In ArcCatalog, Normal (Normal.gxt) is the only project that appears in the Project Explorer. There is no default Project in ArcCatalog, and you can't load any templates. You can, of course, add code to Normal.gxt inside modules, class modules, or forms, but again, be careful when making changes.

Once you've invoked the Visual Basic Editor, you can insert a module, class module, or user form. Then you insert a procedure or enter code for an existing event procedure in the item's Code window, where you can write, display, and edit code. You can open as many Code windows as you have modules, class modules, and user forms, so you can easily view the code and copy and paste between Code windows. In addition to creating your own modules, you can import other modules, class modules, or user forms from disk.

If your work requires it, you can add an external object library or type library reference to your project. This makes another application's objects available in your code. Once a reference is set, the referenced objects are displayed in the development environment's Object Browser.

Getting started with VBA

To begin programming with VBA in ArcMap or ArcCatalog, you start the Visual Basic Editor.

To start the Visual Basic Editor

1. Start ArcMap or ArcCatalog.

2. In the Tools menu, select Macros and then Visual Basic Editor.

   You can also use the shortcut keys Alt+F11 to display the Visual Basic Editor.

To navigate among the projects in the Visual Basic Editor, use the Project Explorer. It displays a list of the document's modules, class modules, and user forms.

To add a macro to a module

ArcMap and ArcCatalog both provide a shortcut for creating a simple macro in a module.

1. Click the Tools menu, point to Macros, and then click Macros.

2. Type the name of the macro you want to create in the Macro name text box.

   If you don't specify a module name, the application stores the macro in a module named NewMacros. Preceding a macro's name with a name and a dot stores it in a module with the specified name. If the module doesn't exist, the application creates it.

3. Click the dropdown arrow of the Macros in the combo box and choose the VBA project in which you want to create the macro.

4. Press the Enter key or click Create.

   The stub for a Sub procedure for the macro appears in the Code window.

Adding modules and class modules

All ArcMap and ArcCatalog documents contain the class module ThisDocument, a custom object that represents the specific document associated with a VBA project. The document object is called MxDocument in ArcMap and GxDocument in ArcCatalog. The IDocument interface provides access to the document's title, type, accelerator table, command bars collection, parent application, and Visual Basic project.

Modules and class modules can contain more than one type of procedure: sub, function, or property. You can choose the procedure type and its scope when you insert a procedure. Inserting a procedure is like creating a code template into which you enter code.

Every procedure has either private or public scope. Procedures with private scope are limited to the module that contains them—only a procedure within the same module can call a private procedure. If you declare the procedure as public, other programs and modules can call them.

Variables in your procedures may either be local or global. Global variables exist during the entire time the code executes, whereas local variables exist only while the procedure in which they are declared is running. The next time you execute a procedure, all local variables are reinitialized. However, you can preserve the value of all local variables in a procedure for the code's lifetime by declaring them as static, thereby fixing their value.

To add a procedure to an existing module

1. In the Project Explorer, double-click the ArcMap Objects, ArcCatalog Objects, or Modules folder and then choose the name of the module.

2. Click the Insert menu and click Procedure.

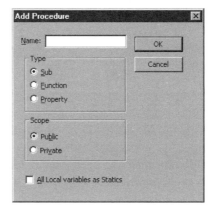

3. In the Name box, name the procedure.

4. From the Type options, select the type of procedure: Sub, Function, or Property.

5. From the Scope options, select either Public or Private.

6. To declare all local variables as static, check All Local variables as Statics.

7. Click OK.

   VBA stubs in a procedure into the item's Code window into which you can enter code. The stub contains the first and last lines of code for the type of procedure you've added.

8. Enter code into the procedure.

See the Microsoft Visual Basic online help reference for more information about procedures.

Adding user forms

If you want your code to prompt the user for information or you want to display the result of some action performed when the user invokes an ArcMap or ArcCatalog command or tool or in response to some other event, you can make use of VBA's user forms. User forms provide a context in which you can provide access to a rich set of integrable controls. Some of these controls are similar to the UIControls that are available as part of the Customize dialog's Commands tab. In addition to text boxes or command buttons, you have access to a rich set of additional controls. A *user form* is a container for user interface controls such as command buttons and text boxes. A *control* is a Visual Basic object you place on a user form that has its own properties, methods, and events. You use controls to receive user input, display output, and trigger event procedures. You can set the form to be either *modal,* in which case the user must respond before using any other part of the application, or *modeless,* in which case subsequent code is executed as it's encountered.

To add and start coding in a user form

1. In the Project Explorer, select the Project to which you want to add a user form.

2. In the Insert menu click UserForm.

   VBA inserts a user form into your project and opens the Controls Toolbox.

3. Select the controls that you want to add to the user form from the Controls Toolbox.

4. Add code to the user form or to its controls.

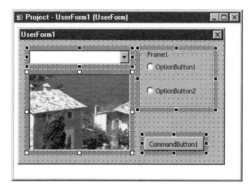

See the Microsoft Visual Basic online help reference for more information about adding controls.

To display the Code window for a user form or control, double-click the user form or control. Then choose the event you want your code to trigger from the dropdown list of events and procedures in the Code window and start typing your code. Or, just as in a module or class module, insert a procedure and start typing your code.

To display the form during an ArcMap or ArcCatalog session in response to some action, you'll invoke its Show method, for example:

```
UserForm1.Show 0 'show modeless
```

Some VBA project management techniques

To work efficiently in the ArcMap or ArcCatalog VBA development environment and reduce the amount of work you have to do every time you start a new task, you can make use of several techniques that will streamline your work:

• Reuse modules, class modules, and user forms.

• Remove unused project items.

• Lock your code, if necessary, from being viewed or modified by users.

Reusing modules, class modules, and user forms

To add an existing module or form to the Normal template, the Project, or a TemplateProject, click the name of the destination in the Project Explorer and then choose Import File from the File menu. You can choose any VBA module, user form, or class module to add a copy of the file to your project. To export an item from your project so that it will be available for importing into other projects, select the item you want to export in the Project Explorer, then choose Export File from the File menu, and then navigate to where you want to save the file. Exporting an item does not remove it from your project.

Removing project items

When you remove an item, it is permanently deleted from the project list—you can't undo the Remove action; however, this action doesn't delete a file if it exists on disk. Before removing an item, make sure remaining code in other modules and user forms doesn't refer to code in the removed item. To remove an item, select it in the Project Explorer and then choose Remove <Name> from the File menu. Before you remove the item, you'll be asked whether you want to export it. If you click Yes in the message box,

the Export File dialog box opens. If you click No, VBA deletes the item.

Protecting your code

To protect your code from alteration and viewing by users, you can lock a Project, a TemplateProject, or even Normal. When you lock one of these items, you set a password that must be entered before it can be viewed in the Project Explorer. To lock one of these items, right-click Project, TemplateProject, or Normal in the Project Explorer and then click the Properties item in the context menu that appears. In the Properties dialog click the Protection tab and select Lock Project for Viewing. Enter a password and confirm it. Finally, save your ArcMap or ArcCatalog file and close it. The next time you or anyone else opens the file, the project is locked. If anyone wants to view or edit the project, they must enter the password.

Saving a VBA project

VBA projects are stored in a file that can be an ArcMap base template (*.mxt), the Normal template (Normal.mxt or Normal.gxt), or an ArcMap document (*.mxd). When a user creates a new ArcMap document from a base template, the new document references the base template's VBA project and its items. To save your ArcMap document and your VBA project, choose Save from the ArcMap File menu or Save <File Name> from the File menu in the Visual Basic Editor. Both commands save your file with the project and any items stored in it. After saving the file, its file name is displayed in the Project Explorer in parentheses after the project name. To save the document as a template choose Save As from the ArcMap File menu and specify ArcMap Templates (*.mxt) as the File type.

Running VBA code

As you build and refine your code, you can run it within VBA to test and debug it. This section discusses running your code in the Visual Basic Editor during design time. See Microsoft Visual Basic online help for more information about running and debugging a VBA program such as adding breakpoints, adding watch expressions, and stepping into and out of execution.

To run your code in the Visual Basic Editor or from the Macros dialog box

1. From the Tools menu, choose Macros.

2. In the Macro list, select the macro you want and then click Run.

If the macro you want is not listed, make sure you've chosen the appropriate item: either Normal, Project, or TemplateProject in the Macros In box. Private procedures do not appear in any menus or dialog boxes.

To run only one procedure in the Visual Basic Editor

1. In the Project Explorer, open the module that contains the procedure that you want to run.

2. In the Code window, click an insertion point in the procedure code.

3. From the Run menu, choose Run Sub/UserForm.

   Only the procedure in which your cursor is located runs.

After you've finished writing your code

After you have finished writing code, users can run it from ArcMap or ArcCatalog. To do this, they choose Macros and then Macros from the Tools menu. Or you can associate the code with a command or tool, or it can run in response to events or in other ways that you design.

Working with Visual Basic

In the previous sections of this chapter, this book focused primarily on how to write code in the Visual Basic for Applications (VBA) development environment embedded within ArcMap and ArcCatalog. This section focuses on particular issues related to creating ActiveX DLLs that can be added to the applications and writing external standalone applications that control ESRI applications using the Visual Basic development environment.

Creating COM components

Most developers will use Visual Basic to create a COM component that works with ArcMap or ArcCatalog. If you worked with the tutorial in Chapter 2, you learned that since the ESRI applications are COM clients—their architecture supports the use of software components that adhere to the COM specification—you can build components with different languages including Visual Basic. These components can then be added to the applications easily. For information about packaging and deploying COM components that you've built with Visual Basic, see Chapter 10, 'Building and delivering extensions'. If you didn't work with the COM component section of the tutorial, you may want to do so now.

In Visual Basic you can build a COM component that will work with ArcMap or ArcCatalog by creating an ActiveX DLL. We'll review the rudimentary steps involved. Note that these steps are not all-inclusive. Your project may involve other requirements.

1. Start Visual Basic. In the New Project dialog create an ActiveX DLL Project.

2. In the Properties window, make sure that the Instancing property for the initial class module and any other class modules you add to the Project are set to 5 - MultiUse:

3. Reference the Object Libraries.

   Specify the appropriate ESRI object libraries to provide information to Visual Basic about the interfaces, coclasses, enumerations, properties, and methods you can use.

4. Implement the required interfaces.

   When you implement an interface in a class module, the class provides its own versions of all the Public procedures specified in the type library of the Interface. In addition to providing a mapping between the interface prototypes and your procedures, the Implements statement causes the class to accept COM QueryInterface calls for the specified interface ID.

You must include all the Public procedures involved. A missing member in an implementation of an interface or class causes an error. If you don't put code in one of the procedures in a class you are implementing, you can raise the appropriate error (Const E_NOTIMPL = &H80004001). That way, if someone else uses the class, they'll understand that a member is not implemented.

5. Add any additional code that's needed.

6. Establish the Project Name and other properties to identify the component.

   In the Project Properties dialog the Project Name you specify will be used as the name of the component's type library. It can be combined with the name of each class the component provides to produce unique class names (these names are also called ProgIDs). These names appear in the Component Category Manager.

7. Compile the DLL.

8. Set the component's Version Compatibility.

   As your code evolves it's good practice to set the components to Binary Compatibility so if you make changes to a component, you'll be warned that you're breaking compatibility. For additional information, see the 'Binary compatilbility mode' help topic in the Visual Basic online help.

9. Recompile the DLL.

10. Make the component available to the application.

   You can add a component to a document or template by clicking the Add from file button in the Customize Dialog's

Commands tab. In addition, you can register a component in the Component Category Manager.

Setting references to the ESRI object libraries

The principle difference between working with the VBA development environment embedded in the applications and working with Visual Basic is that the latter environment requires that you load the appropriate object libraries so that any object variables that you declare can be found. If you don't add the reference, you'll get this error message:

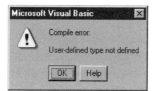

To add a reference to an object library

In all cases, you'll need to load the ESRI Object Library (esriCore.olb). Depending on what you want your code to do, you may add other ESRI object libraries such as the ESRI ArcMap Object Library (esriMx.olb) or the ESRI ArcCatalog Object Library (esriGx.olb).

To display the References dialog box in which you can set the references you need, select References in the Visual Basic Project menu.

After you set a reference to an object library by selecting the check box next to its name, you can find a specific object and its methods and properties in the Object Browser.

If you are not using any objects in a referenced library, you should clear the check box for that reference to minimize the number of object references Visual Basic must resolve, thus reducing the time it takes your project to compile. You can't remove a reference for an item that is used in your project.

You can't remove the "Visual Basic for Applications" and "Visual Basic objects and procedures" references because they are necessary for running Visual Basic.

Referring to a document

Each VBA project (i.e., Normal, Project, TemplateProject) has a class called ThisDocument, which represents the document object. Anywhere you write code in VBA you can reference the document as ThisDocument. Further, if you are writing your code in the ThisDocument Code window, you have direct access to all the methods and properties on IDocument. This is not available in Visual Basic. You must first get a reference to the Application and then the document, for example:

```
Dim m_doc as IDocument
Set m_doc = pApp.Document 'where pApp is a
                          'variable set to the
                          'Application object
```

Creating an instance of ArcMap

If you plan to write an external program that controls ArcMap or ArcCatalog through Automation, you must write code to interact with an instance of one of these programs. To manage instances of ArcMap or ArcCatalog, you register an object in the running object table. A running object table is a globally accessible table on each computer that keeps track of all COM objects in the running state that can be identified by a *moniker*. A moniker is an object that acts as a name that uniquely identifies a COM object. In the same way that a path identifies a file in the file system, a moniker identifies a COM object in the directory namespace. To facilitate this, the ESRI object library provides an Application Running Object Table (AppROT) object.

To create an instance of ArcMap

Unlike other Automation servers, creating a running instance of ArcMap requires that you create a Document object first, which in turn creates the application. Here's an example:

```
Dim m_Doc as IDocument
Sub StartArcMap()
    If m_doc Is Nothing Then
        Set m_doc = New MxDocument 'start ArcMap
    End If
End Sub
```

Once you have the Document, you can use Parent property of the Document to get a reference to the Application object.

To see if an instance is already running

You can use AppROT's Count property to determine whether one of the applications is already running, in which case the reference count will be greater than 0. You can then use the TypeOf keyword to determine whether the application reference returned by the Item property refers to ArcMap or ArcCatalog, for example:

```
Dim WithEvents m_appRot As AppROT
Sub CheckInstance()
   Set m_appRot = New AppROT
   If m_appRot.Count > 0 Then
      For i = 0 To m_appRot.Count - 1
        If TypeOf m_appRot.Item(i) _
          Is IGxApplication Then
          MsgBox "ArcCatalog is already running"
        ElseIf TypeOf m_appRot.Item(i) _
          Is IMxApplication Then
          MsgBox "ArcMap is already running"
```

```
      End If
    Next i
  End If
End Sub
```

To shut down an instance of ArcMap

Halting a running instance of ArcMap from a running program involves shutting down the application and releasing the Document. In the example that follows, Parent references the application object.

```
Sub QuitArcMap()
  If m_doc Is Nothing Then
    Exit Sub
  Else
    m_doc.Parent.Shutdown 'quit ArcMap
    Set m_doc = Nothing 'release m_doc
  End If
End Sub
```

Running ArcMap with a command line argument

You can start ArcMap from the command line and pass it an argument that is either the pathname of a document (.mxd) or the pathname of a template (*.mxt). In the former case ArcMap will open the document; in the latter case ArcMap will create a new document based on the template specified.

You can also pass an argument and create an instance of ArcMap by supplying arguments to the Win32 API's ShellExecute function or Visual Basic's Shell function, as follows:

```
Dim ret As Variant
ret = Shell("d:\arcexe80\bin\arcmap.exe _
d:\arcexe80\bin\templates\LetterPortrait.mxt", _
vbNormalFocus)
```

By default, Shell runs other programs asynchronously. This means that ArcMap might not finish executing before the statements following the Shell function are executed.

To execute a program and wait until it is terminated, you must call three Win32 API functions. First, call the CreateProcessA function to load and execute ArcMap. Next, call the WaitForSingleObject function, which forces the operating system to wait until ArcMap has been terminated. Finally, when the user has terminated the application, call the CloseHandle function to release the application's 32-bit identifier to the system pool.

Working with the Customization Framework 5

This chapter provides information on how to interact and enhance the elements of the ESRI Object library that relate to the Customization Framework. Typically, users interact with the Customization Framework to do the following:

- Create or modify commands, tools, and toolbars to provide an application-specific or user-specific user interface in which to work with the application and its document.

- Lock the state of customizations or disable access to proprietary code.

Templates

What is a template?

A template is simply an ArcMap document file intended as a starting point for other documents. Templates can contain references to data, symbolsets, various settings, and customizations such as custom toolbars, menus, and accelerators. In addition, each template contains its own VBA project, which can contain Visual Basic Subroutines, Functions, forms and controls, modules, and classes. This section will discuss those aspects of templates specifically related to user customizations and VBA.

Creating template documents

When you create a new document, you can base your document on one of the existing templates provided with ArcMap. You can create your own templates by using the Save As menu selection to save the current document as a template. When a template-based ArcMap document is loaded, the template file is also loaded. This powerful feature allows dynamic updates to customizations stored in these templates since any existing documents based on the same template are also updated.

The Normal template

In addition to any specific template, a document is always based on a special template called Normal. The Normal template is the global template as it contains those customizations and VBA code that you want available to all documents. The Normal template is automatically loaded with all ArcMap documents including brand new documents created with the New menu choice. The Normal template is always called Normal.mxt and can be located in your Templates directory. Note that ArcCatalog does not follow the same template model as ArcMap. ArcCatalog only has a Normal template, named Normal.gxt, and no document or base template.

Accessing templates from VBA projects

As mentioned previously, each document or template file has an associated VBA project. The VBA project for each file is named consistently by default: The primary document file is called Project; the base template file, if present, is called ProjectTemplate. Finally, the Normal template file's VBA project is called Normal. When writing VBA code, you can programmatically access macros and other objects in loaded templates by prefixing such requests with the Project name. For instance, you can call a subroutine called HelloWorld in the Normal project from the Project with the following VBA snippet:

```
Sub Test 'In Project
    'Call subroutine HelloWorld in Normal.
    Call Normal.HelloWorld

    'Set the caption of a form in the project
    'template.
    ProjectTemplate.Form1.Caption = "Test"
End Sub
```

Note that it isn't necessary to prefix objects with the scope name if both the code and the object exist in the same VBA project.

Customization context

The currently loaded document file and each of its associated templates can be thought of as layers in a stack. The Normal template is loaded first and so forms the base of this stack. The project template, if specified, is loaded next; note that documents are created without a project template by default. Finally, the primary document file is loaded and forms the top level of the stack.

Customizations are done in the context of one of these levels. The Save In combobox located in the lower-left portion of the Customization dialog controls which level subsequent Customizations are associated with. The ordering of these levels is significant since higher level templates have the ability to override customizations made in lower level templates. For instance, let's say you have a commonly executed script (macro) stored in Normal's VBA project. You would like to make it easier to execute this macro, so you decide to place a button on the standard toolbar, which launches this script. Finally, you want this button to be visible in all your documents, that is, all existing documents and any new ones you might create in the future. You can do this by first displaying the Customize dialog and selecting Normal in the Save In combobox, since in this case you want to associate the change with Normal (the global template). Then, simply drag and drop the appropriate macro from the Commands page—in the Macros category—onto the standard toolbar. Exit the Customize dialog and you're done! If you wanted the button to appear in the document you were working on exclusively, you would select the document name in the Save In combobox instead.

Resetting customizations

There may be times when you want to undo any customizations you've made. This is again made in the context of a specific template level. Selecting Reset erases any previous customizations made in the selected context.

Programmatic customizations

The template model allows for flexible customization through the user interface with an easy drag-and-drop paradigm. The model also provides an easy way to make global updates and modifications, since template files are shared between other documents, and creates the conditions optimal for VBA code

reuse. Finally, the template model automatically merges and coordinates changes made in each of the loaded levels. There are, however, times when you may want to make customizations that are based on the state of the system or when some key action is taken by the user of the document. This is where programmatic customizations come into play.

A programmatic customization is made by writing code that manipulates various customization-related objects instead of utilizing the user interface. Unlike customizations made through the user interface, *the results of programmatic customizations are not persistent*, that is, they do not reappear the next time the document is opened because programmatic customizations are intended for dynamic cases that do not fit well into the template-based (and persistent) customization model. The code that causes these changes must be rerun whenever the document is opened.

The document object

Each VBA project contains a VBA class called ThisDocument. This class, as the name implies, represents the ArcMap document itself. Note that each VBA project contains its own ThisDocument class, which represents that project's template. The document object acts as the doorway to other parts of the object model such as the Accelerators, CommandBars, Maps, and Display and Application objects.

Document events

The document object also exposes a number of events through the IDocumentEventsDisp Interface. These events fire when you take various actions as indicated in the following table:

Event	Fired
ActiveViewChanged	...when you change the active view.
BeforeCloseDocument	...before you close a document. Return True to abort the close process.
CloseDocument	...when you close the document.
MapsChanged	...when you make a change to the map collection.
NewDocument	...when you create a new document.
OnContextMenu	...when you click the right mouse button to display a context menu at the given x,y location. Return True to indicate that a custom context menu has handled the event.
OpenDocument	...when you open the document.

Locking and customization filters

The ability to customize the user interface is a powerful feature of any software. Specialized documents may want to restrict the extent to which users of the document are able to customize. ArcMap can be locked so that certain restrictions are applied including the ability to invoke the Customize dialog or the ability to access the VBA environment. ArcMap can be locked from the Customize dialog or programmatically using a password. Note that VBA code modules can be individually locked for reading using a similar fashion. Customization filters are advanced features whereby fine-grained restrictions can be applied. For instance, you can control exactly which categories and commands are presented to the document user from the Customize dialog. Customization filters can only be applied programmatically.

The Customization Framework object model

The objects in the Customization Framework part of the ArcInfo Object Model allow you to programmatically customize the user interface in ArcMap and ArcCatalog. You can modify the built-in toolbars and commands, or you can create your own custom toolbars and commands.

The Application object is the core object in the ArcMap and ArcCatalog applications. This object represents the application itself and acts as the central point where access is gained to other objects in the system. The Application object's primary interface is IApplication. This interface provides access to the Document object, the StatusBar object, the Templates object, the currently selected tool, and the Visual Basic Editor. There are several methods that allow you to open, save, and print documents, lock and unlock the application from user customizations, display dialogs, and exit the application. When working within the integrated VBA environment, the Application object is exposed globally. That means you can directly access the properties and methods of the application from any routine without first obtaining a reference to that object.

The Templates object is a collection of the templates that are currently loaded in the application. In ArcCatalog, the Normal template, Normal.gxt, is the only template that is ever loaded. In ArcMap, there are either two or three templates loaded. The Normal template, Normal.mxt, is always loaded. Also, the document is considered a template is this case; there is always a document loaded in ArcMap. Optionally, the document can be based on another template referred to as a base template. The ITemplates interface allows you to get a count of the loaded templates and get the pathnames of those templates. Use IApplication::Templates to get a reference to the templates collection.

The StatusBar is the horizontal area at the bottom of the ArcMap or ArcCatalog application window. The StatusBar provides information about the current state of what you are doing in the application. The IStatusBar interface allows you to set the properties of the StatusBar. Use IApplication::StatusBar to get a reference to the StatusBar.

The Document object is called MxDocument in ArcMap and GxDocument in ArcCatalog. The IDocument interface provides access to the document's title, type, accelerator table, CommandBars collection, parent application, and Visual Basic project. Use IApplication::Document to get a reference to the document.

An Accelerator is a mapping between a particular keyboard combination and a command. When you press the combination of keys on the keyboard, the command is executed. For example, Ctrl-C is a well-known accelerator for copying something in Windows. Some commands in the application already have accelerators assigned to them, but you can also assign additional accelerators to these commands. The IAccelerator interface defines the properties of an accelerator. Use the IAcceleratorTable::Add method to create an accelerator.

The AcceleratorTable is an object that contains a list of accelerator keys and the command identifiers associated with them. The IAcceleratorTable interface is used to add or find accelerators in an AcceleratorTable. You can get a reference to the AcceleratorTable of a document using IDocument::Accelerators.

A CommandBar is a toolbar, a menubar, menu, or a context menu. With the ICommandBar interface you can modify a CommandBar such as adding a command, menu, or macro item to it. Use ICommandBars::Find to get a reference to a particular CommandBar.

CommandBars is a collection of all the toolbars available to a document. The ICommandBars interface allows you to set properties for the CommandBars and to create, find, or hide CommandBars. Use IDocument::CommandBars to get a reference to the CommandBars collection.

A CommandItem is any item on a CommandBar. For example, button, tools, and menu items that appear on CommandBars are all CommandItems. The ICommandItem interface allows you to get or set the properties of the CommandItem such as caption, button image, StatusBar message, tooltip, display style, help context ID, and more. You can obtain a reference to the command on which this item is based. The ICommandItem interface also provides methods to execute, delete, refresh, and reset the CommandItem. Use either ICommandBars::Find or ICommandBar::Find to obtain a reference to a particular CommandItem.

Custom commands

As a developer you may want to add functionality to the ArcMap and ArcCatalog applications by creating custom commands. There are three basic types of commands that you can create:

- COM commands
- Macro items
- UIControls

COM commands

You can create COM commands in any development environment that supports COM, for example, Visual Basic, C++, J++, or Delphi™. COM-based commands are distributed in the form of ActiveX DLLs. You can create the following types of commands:

Buttons and menu items are the simplest types of commands. Buttons generally appear as icons on toolbars, and menu items

appear in menus. A simple action is performed when the button or menu item is clicked.

Tools are similar to buttons, but they also require interaction with the application's display. The Zoom In command is a good example of a tool—you click or drag a rectangle over a map before the display is redrawn to show the map contents in more detail.

Tool controls are commands that act like comboboxes or editboxes. Comboboxes let you choose an option from a drop-down list. For example, in ArcMap you can choose which layer(s) you are selecting features from when working with a map. Editboxes are editable textboxes where you can type in text.

To create a custom COM command, you would implement some of the ArcObjects interfaces that support commands such as ICommand, ITool, IToolControl, ICommandSubType, and IMultiItem.

The ICommand interface must be implemented by all COM-based commands (except for MultiItems). This interface determines the behavior and properties of simple commands such as buttons and menu items. For example, the ICommand interface sets command properties such as caption, name, category, bitmap, StatusBar message, tooltip, help context ID and help file, enabled state, and checked state. It also defines what action happens when the command is clicked.

The ITool interface is implemented by specialized commands that can interact with the application's display. Only one tool can be active in the application at a time. With the ITool interface you can define what occurs on events such as mouse move, mouse button press/release, keyboard key press/release, double-click, and right-click.

The IToolControl interface is implemented by commands that act as editbox controls or combobox controls. A command that implements IToolControl passes its window handle to the application.

The ICommandSubType interface is used when you want to have more than one command in a single class. You would implement both ICommand and ICommandSubType in your class. With the ICommandSubType interface you would specify how many subtypes there are. Then, within the implementation of each ICommand property, you would set the property for each subtype instead of implementing the ICommand interface multiple times.

A MultiItem can be used when items on a menu can't be determined prior to run time or the items need to be modified based on the state of the system. A good example of this is the menu items at the bottom of the File menu representing the most recently used files. The IMultiItem interface allows a single object to act like several adjacent menu items. During run time, the framework will notify MultiItem commands when their host menu is about to be shown. At this point, all the commands implementing IMultiItem can query the system to determine how many items should be represented and how each should appear. The IMultiItem interface allows you to assign properties such as caption, bitmap, enabled state, and checked state to each item. You do not implement the ICommand interface when creating a MultiItem.

Macro items

Macro items are VBA based. This means that they are created using the Visual Basic environment that is embedded in the applications. Macros are simple Sub procedures written in the Visual Basic Editor. Macro items can be created from these macros by dragging them onto any toolbar.

UIControls

UIControls are also VBA based. The types of UIControls that you can create include UIButtonControls, UIToolControls, UIEditBoxControls, and UIComboboxControls.

A UIButtonControl acts as a button or menu item that performs a simple task when clicked. You can set properties such as StatusBar message, tooltip, enabled state, and checked state.

A UIToolControl is similar to a COM command that implements the ITool interface. This type of control can interact with the application's display. You can set all the properties that UIButtonControls have and also define what occurs on events such as mouse move, mouse button press/release, keyboard key press/release, double-click, and right-click.

A UIEditBoxControl is an editable textbox control that can be added to a toolbar. There is a property to set the text that appears in the editbox. The Change and Keydown events allow you to control what happens when a user changes the text in the editbox.

A UIComboboxControl is a dropdown list box control that can be added to a toolbar. There are properties and methods that allow you to change, add, and remove items in the combobox list. The EditChange, SelectionChange, and Keydown event allow you to control what happens when a user changes the text or selection in the combobox.

Custom COM toolbars and menus

You may want to create custom toolbars and menus in order to organize commands in a meaningful manner. You can create COM-based CommandBars in any development environment that supports COM, for example, Visual Basic, C++, J++, or Delphi. COM-based CommandBars are distributed in the form of ActiveX DLLs. To create a custom toolbar you would implement

IToolbarDef, and to create a custom menu you would implement IMenuDef.

The IToolbarDef interface is used to define the properties of a custom toolbar. You can set the caption and name of the toolbar and specify what commanditems are on the toolbar.

The IMenuDef interface is identical to the IToolbarDef interface except that it is used to indicate to the application that this is a menu. If you are creating a context menu, you would implement both IMenuDef and IShortcutMenu. IShortcutMenu is an indicator interface that is used only to indicate to the application that this menu should be treated as a context menu.

Using VBA macros to control customizations

You can use VBA macros for a variety of customization framework tasks including controlling execution of a built-in command, setting the active tool, and creating menus and menu items.

In each of these macros, the built-in ArcID module is used to find the ArcMap commands.

The ExecuteCmd macro executes Zoom to Full Extent in ArcMap.

The ActivateTool macro makes the Identify tool the currently active tool in ArcMap.

The CreateToolbar macro creates a new toolbar called MyToolBar in ArcMap and then adds the ArcMap AddData and ZoomFullExtent commands to the toolbar. The code docks the toolbar on the right side of the application.

The CreateMenu macro shows how to add a new menu to the Main Menu bar in ArcMap and add items to it. The ArcMap Add Data command is added to the new menu. Then the sample macro MyMacro is added as an item on the new menu. ▶

```vba
Sub ExecuteCmd()
    Dim pItem As ICommandItem
    Set pItem = Project.ThisDocument.CommandBars.Find _
        (ArcID.PanZoom_FullExtent)
    pItem.Execute
End Sub


Sub ActivateTool()
    Dim pItem As ICommandItem
    Set pItem = Project.ThisDocument.CommandBars.Find _
        (ArcID.Query_Identify)
    Set Application.CurrentTool = pItem
End Sub


Public Sub CreateToolBar()
    Dim pCmdBar As ICommandBar
    Set pCmdBar = CommandBars.Create("MyToolBar", esriCmdBarTypeToolbar)
    pCmdBar.Add ArcID.File_AddData
    pCmdBar.Add ArcID.PanZoom_FullExtent
    pCmdBar.Dock (esriDockRight)
End Sub


Public Sub CreateMenu()
    'Find the MainMenubar.
    Dim pMainMenubar As ICommandBar
    Set pMainMenubar = ThisDocument.CommandBars.Find(ArcID.MainMenu)

    'Create the new menu called "MyMenu" on the MainMenubar.
    Dim pNewMenu As ICommandBar
    Set pNewMenu = pMainMenubar.CreateMenu("MyMenu")
```

The AssignAccelerator macro shows how to programmatically assign a keyboard accelerator to a command. In this example, the keyboard accelerator Ctrl+A is assigned the Add Data command in ArcMap.

Tip

The life span of customizations

All programmatic customizations are temporary. If you customize ArcMap programmatically, these changes will only appear while the current document is open in the current ArcMap session. Programmatic changes are never saved in the document or templates. Once you close that document or exit ArcMap, the changes are removed. If you are customizing ArcCatalog, these changes will only appear during the current ArcCatalog session.

```
'Add a built in command to the new menu.
pNewMenu.Add ArcID.File_AddData

'Add a macro to the new menu.
'The macro item's name will be "MyMacroItem",
'it'll have an icon of a happy face (the 1st bitmap image),
'and will fire a macro called "MyMacro" (provided below).
pNewMenu.CreateMacroItem "MyMacroItem", 1, _
    Normal.ThisDocument.MyMacro"
End Sub

Public Sub MyMacro()
    'This is the macro that is added to the new menu.
    MsgBox ("I know how to create a new menu and a new macro item!")
End Sub

Public Sub AssignAccelerator()
    Dim addedAcc As Boolean
    addedAcc = ThisDocument.Accelerators.Add _
    (ArcID.File_AddData, vbKeyA, True, False, False)
End Sub
```

Creating a shortcut menu

You can use the Visual Basic Editor to create a shortcut or so-called context menu. The context menu can take precedence over an existing context menu. Shortcut menus are available by right-clicking the mouse in a specific context. In this case, the function named MxDocument_OnContextMenu, a built-in event procedure, displays a new shortcut menu when you right-click the Data View in ArcMap. This function creates the shortcut menu on the fly, adds some built-in ArcMap commands and a submenu to it, and then pops the menu up. By setting the value of the function to True at the end of the Function, you prevent the built-in context menu from appearing after the custom shortcut menu displays.

```
Private Function MxDocument_OnContextMenu(ByVal X As Long, ByVal Y As Long) As Boolean
  ' Create a shortcut menu.
  Dim pShortcutMenu As ICommandBar
  Set pShortcutMenu = CommandBars.Create("MyShortcutMenu", _
  esriCmdBarTypeShortcutMenu)
  ' Add 3 built in commands to the new shortcut menu
  With pShortcutMenu
    .Add ArcID.PanZoom_Up
    .Add ArcID.PanZoom_Down
    .Add ArcID.PanZoom_PageLeft
    .Add ArcID.PanZoom_PageRight
    ' Create a sub-menu called "MySubMenu" on the new shortcut menu.
    ' The second argument to CreateMenu, 2, is the index that
    ' represents the sub-menu's position. Since the index is 0-based,
    ' the sub-menu will be positioned as the third item.
    Dim pSubMenu As ICommandBar
    Set pSubMenu = .CreateMenu("MySubMenu", 2)
    ' Add a few items to the sub-menu.
    With pSubMenu
      .Add ArcID.PanZoom_ZoomInFixed
      .Add ArcID.PanZoom_FullExtent
      .Add ArcID.PanZoom_ZoomOutFixed
    End With
    ' Pop the shortcut menu up.
    .Popup
  End With
  ' Handled
  MxDocument_OnContextMenu = True
End Function
```

Creating a custom tool and custom toolbar

Creating a tool to interact with some aspect of the application as it appears on the screen is at the heart of interactive development.

Here we create a custom tool, MyTool, and custom toolbar, MyToolbar, using Visual Basic. This custom tool illustrates when certain mouse and keyboard events occur by displaying a message box or a message in the status bar when each event is fired. For example, when you click on the tool, a message box is displayed. The StatusBar message will change when you move the mouse, press or release the left mouse button, or press or release a key on the keyboard. If you double-click, the Select Graphics Tool will become the active tool. If you right-click, a custom context menu will be displayed.

The class for MyTool implements the ICommand and ITool interfaces. To create any type of command in Visual Basic for use in ArcInfo, you need to implement ICommand. Since we are creating a tool here, we also need to implement the ITool interface. Even if you don't need to write ▶

```vb
Option Explicit

' Implement the ICommand and ITool interfaces
Implements ICommand
Implements ITool

Dim pApp As esriMx.Application        'ArcMap application
Dim m_pBitmap As IPictureDisp         'Bitmap for the command
Dim m_pCursor As IPictureDisp         'Cursor for the command


Private Sub Class_Initialize()
   'Load the button image and cursor from the resource file.
   Set m_pBitmap = LoadResPicture(105, 0)
   Set m_pCursor = LoadResPicture(110, 2)
End Sub


Private Property Get ICommand_Bitmap() As esriCore.OLE_HANDLE
   ' Set the bitmap of the command. The m_pBitmap variable is set
   ' in Class_Initialize.
   ICommand_Bitmap = m_pBitmap
End Property


Private Property Get ICommand_Caption() As String
   ' Set the string that appears when the command is used as a
   ' menu item.
   ICommand_Caption = "MyTool"
End Property
```

code for all the properties and events on these interfaces to meet the requirements of your command design, you must at least create stub code for all of the properties and events.

The bitmap and cursor for the tool are loaded from a resource file that is included in the Visual Basic project. An alternative way to store the bitmap and cursor is to create a VB form and add a PictureBox for the bitmap and a PictureBox for the cursor to it.

The class for MyToolbar implements the IToolbarDef interface. This custom toolbar has the custom tool MyTool on it in addition to two of the ArcMap built-in commands.

```vb
Private Property Get ICommand_Category() As String
    ' Set the category of this command. This determines where the
    ' command appears in the Commands panel of the Customize dialog.
    ICommand_Category = "MyCoolTool"
End Property

Private Property Get ICommand_Checked() As Boolean
End Property

Private Property Get ICommand_Enabled() As Boolean
    ' Add some logic here to specify when the command should
    ' be in for command to be enabled. In this example, the command
    ' is always enabled.
    ICommand_Enabled = True
End Property

Private Property Get ICommand_HelpContextID() As Long
End Property

Private Property Get ICommand_HelpFile() As String
End Property

Private Property Get ICommand_Message() As String
    'Set the message string that appears in the StatusBar of the
    'application when the mouse passes over the command.
    ICommand_Message = "This is my cool tool"
End Property
```

```
Private Property Get ICommand_Name() As String
  ' Set the internal name of this command. By convention, this
  ' name string contains the category and caption of the command.
  ICommand_Name = "MyCoolTool_MyTool"
End Property

Private Sub ICommand_OnClick()
  ' Add some code to do some action when the command is clicked. In this
  ' example, a message box is displayed.
  MsgBox "Clicked on my command"
End Sub

Private Sub ICommand_OnCreate(ByVal hook As Object)
  ' The hook argument is a pointer to Application object.
  ' Establish a hook to the application
  Set pApp = hook
End Sub

Private Property Get ICommand_Tooltip() As String
  'Set the string that appears in the screen tip.
  ICommand_Tooltip = "MyTool"
End Property

Private Property Get ITool_Cursor() As esriCore.OLE_HANDLE
  ' Set the cursor of the command. The m_pCursor variable is set
  ' in Class_Initialize
  ITool_Cursor = m_pCursor
End Property
```

```
Private Function ITool_Deactivate() As Boolean
  ' Deactivate the tool. If set to False (the default), you cannot
  ' interact with any other tools because this tool cannot be
  ' interrupted by another tool.
  ITool_Deactivate = True
End Function

Private Function ITool_OnContextMenu(ByVal X As Long, ByVal Y As Long) As
Boolean
  ' Add some code to show a custom context menu when
  ' there is a right click.
  ' This example creates a new context menu with
  Dim pShortCut As ICommandBar
  Dim pitem As ICommandItem
  ' Create a new context menu
  Set pShortCut = pApp.Document.CommandBars.Create("MyShortCut", _
    esriCmdBarTypeShortcutMenu)
  ' Add an item to it
  Set pitem = pShortCut.CreateMacroItem("MyMacro", 7)
  ' Display the menu
  pShortCut.Popup
  ' Let the application know that you handled the OnContextMenu event.
  ' If you don't do this, the standard context menu will be displayed
  ' after this custom context menu.
  ITool_OnContextMenu = True
End Function
```

```
Private Sub ITool_OnDblClick()
    ' Add some code to do some action on double-click.
    ' This example makes the builtin Select Graphics Tool the active tool.
    Dim pSelectTool As ICommandItem
    Dim pCommandBars As ICommandBars
    ' The identifier for the Select Graphics Tool
    Dim u As New UID
    u = "{C22579D1-BC17-11D0-8667-0000F8751720}"
    'Find the Select Graphics Tool
    Set pCommandBars = pApp.Document.CommandBars
    Set pSelectTool = pCommandBars.Find(u)
    'Set the current tool of the application to be the Select Graphics Tool
    Set pApp.CurrentTool = pSelectTool
End Sub


Private Sub ITool_OnKeyDown(ByVal keyCode As Long, ByVal Shift As Long)
    ' Add some code to do some action when a keyboard button is pressed.
    ' This example changes the StatusBar message.
    pApp.StatusBar.Message(0) = "ITool_OnKeyDown"
End Sub


Private Sub ITool_OnKeyUp(ByVal keyCode As Long, ByVal Shift As Long)
    ' Add some code to do some action when a keyboard button is released.
    ' This example changes the StatusBar message.
    pApp.StatusBar.Message(0) = "ITool_OnKeyUp"
End Sub
```

```
Private Sub ITool_OnMouseDown(ByVal Button As Long, ByVal Shift As Long,
ByVal X As Long, ByVal Y As Long)
  ' Add some code to do some action when the mouse button is pressed.
  ' This example changes the StatusBar message.
  pApp.StatusBar.Message(0) = "ITool_OnMouseDown"
End Sub


Private Sub ITool_OnMouseMove(ByVal Button As Long, ByVal Shift As Long,
ByVal X As Long, ByVal Y As Long)
  ' Add some code to do some action when the mouse is moved.
  ' This example changes the StatusBar message.
  pApp.StatusBar.Message(0) = "ITool_OnMouseMove"
End Sub


Private Sub ITool_OnMouseUp(ByVal Button As Long, ByVal Shift As Long,
ByVal X As Long, ByVal Y As Long)
  ' Add some code to do some action when the mouse button is released.
  ' This example changes the StatusBar message.
  pApp.StatusBar.Message(0) = "ITool_OnMouseUp"


End Sub


Private Sub ITool_Refresh(ByVal hDC As esriCore.OLE_HANDLE)


End Sub
```

Creating a custom MultiItem and custom menu

A MultiItem can be used when items on a menu can't be determined prior to run time or the items need to be modified based on the state of the system. A good example of this is the set of menu items that constitute the most recently used (MRU) files list at the bottom of the File menu.

ZoomMulti.cls creates a custom MultiItem, ZoomMulti, and ZoomMenu.cls creates a custom menu, ZoomMenu, using Visual Basic. This zoom MultiItem creates a menu item for each layer in the map. Each menu item zooms to the layer. If the layer is not visible in the map, the menu item for that layer is disabled.

The class for ZoomMulti implements the IMultiItem interface. The IMultiItem interface allows a single object to act like several adjacent menu items. During run time, the framework will notify MultiItem commands when their host menu is about to be shown. At this point, all the commands implementing IMultiItem can query the system to determine how many items should be represented and how each should appear.

```
' ZoomMulti.cls
Option Explicit
' Implement the IMultiItem interface
Implements IMultiItem

Dim pApp As esriMx.Application 'ArcMap application
Dim pMxDoc As IMxDocument      'ArcMap document
Dim pMap As IMap               'Current focus map
Dim pLayerCnt As Long          'Number of layers in the map

Private Property Get IMultiItem_Caption() As String
    IMultiItem_Caption = "ZoomToLayers"
End Property


Private Property Get IMultiItem_HelpContextID() As Long
End Property


Private Property Get IMultiItem_HelpFile() As String
End Property


Private Property Get IMultiItem_ItemBitmap(ByVal Index As Long) As
esriCore.OLE_HANDLE
End Property


Private Property Get IMultiItem_ItemCaption(ByVal Index As Long) As
String
    Dim i As Integer
    ' Loop through the layers in the map
    For i = 0 To pLayerCnt - 1
      ' If the layer's index (i) equals the multiItem's index (Index),
      ' then set the caption of the item to be Zoom to
      If Index = i Then
```

The IMultiItem interface allows you to define how many items are in this MultiItem and assign properties, such as caption, bitmap, enabled state, and checked state, to each item. It also defines what happens when each item is clicked.

The class for ZoomMenu implements the IMenuDef and IRootLevelMenu interfaces. The IMenuDef interface is used to define the properties of a custom menu. You can set the caption and name of the menu and specify what items are on the menu. This custom menu only has the custom zoom MultiItem on it. The IRootLevelMenu interface is an indicator interface that is used only to indicate to the application that the menu should be treated as a root menu. This means that the menu cannot appear on another menu; it can only be put on a toolbar or the menubar. The IRootLevelMenu interface has no members.

Even if you don't need to write code for all the properties and events on these interfaces to meet the requirements of your custom MultiItem and menu design, you must at least create stub code for all of the properties and events.

```
        IMultiItem_ItemCaption = "Zoom to " & pMap.Layer(i).Name
    End If
  Next
End Property


Private Property Get IMultiItem_ItemChecked(ByVal Index As Long) As
Boolean
End Property


Private Property Get IMultiItem_ItemEnabled(ByVal Index As Long) As
Boolean
    Dim i As Integer
    ' Loop through the layers in the map.
    For i = 0 To pLayerCnt - 1
      ' If the layer's index (i) equals the multiItem's index (Index),
      ' then make the item enabled only if the layer is currently visible.
      If Index = i Then
        If pMap.Layer(i).Visible Then
          IMultiItem_ItemEnabled = True
        End If
      End If
    Next
End Property


Private Property Get IMultiItem_Message() As String
    IMultiItem_Message = "Zooms to the layer."
End Property


Private Property Get IMultiItem_Name() As String
    IMultiItem_Name = "ZoomMulti"
End Property
```

```
Private Sub IMultiItem_OnItemClick(ByVal Index As Long)
    Dim i As Integer
    Dim pEnv As IEnvelope
    Dim m_BookMark As IAOIBookmark
    ' Loop through the layers in the map
    For i = 0 To pLayerCnt - 1
        ' If the layer's index (i) equals the multiItem's index (Index),
        ' then zoom to the layer.
        If Index = i Then
            ' Get the spatial-referenced extent of the layer.
            Set pEnv = pMap.Layer(i).AreaOfInterest
            ' Make a new BookMark and set it to the extent of the layer.
            Set m_BookMark = New AOIBookmark
            Set m_BookMark.Location = pEnv
            ' Zoom to the bookmark and refresh the view.
            m_BookMark.ZoomTo pMap
            pMxDoc.ActiveView.Refresh
        End If
    Next
End Sub


Private Function IMultiItem_OnPopup(ByVal hook As Object) As Long
    Set pApp = hook
    ' Get the count of layers in the map.
    Set pMxDoc = pApp.Document
    Set pMap = pMxDoc.FocusMap
    pLayerCnt = pMap.LayerCount
    ' Set the number of items in the multiItem to the number of layers.
    IMultiItem_OnPopup = pLayerCnt
End Function
```

Create the custom menu class in conjunction with implementing IMultiItem because this is the only way to bring a custom MultiItem into the applications. Since MultiItems are never added to the commands list in the Customize dialog, you use the custom menu to provide access to them.

```
' ZoomMenu.cls
Option Explicit


' Implement the IMenuDef and IRootLevelMenu interfaces
Implements IMenuDef
Implements IRootLevelMenu

Private Property Get IMenuDef_Caption() As String
    IMenuDef_Caption = "Zoom Menu"
End Property

Private Sub IMenuDef_GetItemInfo(ByVal pos As Long, ByVal itemDef As
esriCore.IItemDef)
    Select Case pos
    Case 0
      itemDef.ID = "ZoomMultiItem.ZoomMulti"
    End Select
End Sub

Private Property Get IMenuDef_ItemCount() As Long
    IMenuDef_ItemCount = 1
End Property

Private Property Get IMenuDef_Name() As String
    IMenuDef_Name = "ZoomMenu"
End Property
```

Creating a Customization Filter

There may be situations in which you need to prevent or control access to specific types of customization. By combining templates or documents in which specific functionality of the application has been removed with code similar to that given here, you can design a user interface that remains as delivered. The code listed here shows how to use a Customization Filter to lock some of the customization functionality in ArcMap. The lock does the following three things:

1. Prevents the Visual Basic Editor from being opened.

2. Locks the Map and Edit categories. These categories will not appear in the Categories list on the Commands panel of the Customize dialog. This prevents users from dragging the commands in these categories onto toolbars.

3. Locks the What's This Help command. This command will not show up in the Commands list for the Help category on the Commands panel of the Customize dialog. This prevents users from dragging this command onto a toolbar but still gives ▶

```
' MyFilter.cls
Option Explicit
Implements ICustomizationFilter


Private Function ICustomizationFilter_OnCustomizationEvent(ByVal
custEventType As esriCore.esriCustomizationEvent, ByVal eventCtx As
Variant) As Boolean
    ' Lock the Visual Basic editor
    ' custEventType is esriCEShowVBAIDE
    ' eventCtx is nothing
    If custEventType = esriCEShowVBAIDE Then
        ICustomizationFilter_OnCustomizationEvent = True
    End If


    ' Lock the Map and Edit categories. These categories will not appear
    ' in the Categories list on the Commands panel of the Customize
    ' dialog.
    ' custEventType is esriCEAddCategory
    ' eventCtx is a string representing the category name
    If custEventType = esriCEAddCategory Then
        Select Case eventCtx
            Case "Map"
                ICustomizationFilter_OnCustomizationEvent = True
            Case "Edit"
                ICustomizationFilter_OnCustomizationEvent = True
            Case Else
                ICustomizationFilter_OnCustomizationEvent = False
        End Select
    End If


    ' Lock the What's This Help command. This command will not show up
```

them access to the other commands in the Help category.

The class for MyFilter implements the ICustomizationFilter interface. A CustomizationFilter provides a mechanism to lock parts of the customization functionality in ArcMap. The ICustomizationFilter interface has an OnCustomizationEvent event that gets fired whenever a user attempts any type of customization. There are six types of customization events that can happen. These are defined by the esriCustomizationEvent constants. For each type of customization event type there is an event context. Refer to the table below to see what type of information the event context eventCtx provides.

```
' in the Commands list for the Help category on the Commands panel of
'  the Customize dialog.
' custEventType is esriCEAddCommand
' eventCtx can be either a UID or a string identifier for a command.
If custEventType = esriCEAddCommand Then
    'UID for What's This Help command
    Dim u As New UID
    u = "{81972F0D-388A-11D3-9F57-00C04F6BC61A}"
    If u = eventCtx Then
        ICustomizationFilter_OnCustomizationEvent = True
    End If
End If
End Function
```

custEventType	eventCtx
esriCEAddCategory	string representing category name
esriCEAddCommand	UID or string identifying a command
esriCEShowCustDlg	nothing
esriCEShowVBAIDE	nothing
esriCEInvokeCommand	UID of a command
esriCEShowCustCtxMenu	nothing

To use the customization filter in the OpenDocument event of a document, follow these steps:

1. Start ArcMap and open the Visual Basic Editor.

2. Import MyFilter.cls into Project.

3. Add the adjacent code to MxDocument_OpenDocument event.

4. Save the document and open it again. The lock should be activated.

```
Private Function MxDocument_OpenDocument() As Boolean
    ' Do error checking in case there is already a lock active.
    On Error GoTo lockErr
    Dim CustomFilter As ICustomizationFilter
    Set CustomFilter = New MyFilter
    Application.LockCustomization "mylock", CustomFilter
Exit Function
lockErr:
    MsgBox "There is already an active lock.", , "Lock Error"
End Function
```

Working with ArcMap

6

This chapter provides information on how to interact and enhance the elements of the ESRI Object Library that relate to ArcMap. ArcMap provides users an environment in which to display, browse, query, link, and format their geographic data. Typically, users use ArcMap to do the following:

• Visualize and display data geographically to convey information that meets specific needs.

• Solve complex problems by getting answers to spatial questions such as 'Where is...?', 'How much...?', and 'What if...?'. By allowing spatial relationships such as location, contiguity, proximity, and adjacency to be revealed, patterns become evident and solutions follow.

• Create new spatial data based on existing data or generate new data by enabling capturing devices and other acquisition technologies to interact with the application.

• Prepare and generate hiqh-quality cartographic output for dissemination in a variety of media, either hardcopy or electronic.

• Link a variety of other data, such as photographs, tables, drawings, charts, and other elements, to geographic entities.

To illustrate how to work with the ArcMap elements of the ESRI Object Library, this chapter reviews the central ArcMap object model and other areas of the object model associated with it. In addition, several code examples serve to illustrate the elements in use.

The ArcMap object model

The ArcMap object model describes components comprising the core ArcMap application. These objects are starting points for access to the map document data and how it is displayed and manipulated.

Application Framework

Application is the root object for the running application. Any other object related to the current map document, display environment, or application command functions may be found by starting here.

Its Document property points to an MxDocument object (discussed below), which represents all elements comprising the current map document.

Display points to the AppDisplay object (also see below), which focuses on the screen display of map data.

CurrentTool defines whether a command tool object is active.

The handle of the main application window is hWnd.

VBE is the link to the Visual Basic Editor.

Some methods correspond to Main Menu items common to most Windows applications such as NewDocument, OpenDocument, PrintDocument, and ExitApplication.

When you write an ActiveX DLL to implement a custom command for ArcMap, the parameter passed to your ICommand implementation of OnCreate() (shown as "hook" in the object browser) is a pointer to the IApplication interface of Application.

MxDocument represents the current ArcMap document.

The Maps property is the collection of all Map objects in the ArcMap document. It corresponds to the list of data frames in the Table of Contents window (each data frame is a Map). Map objects are covered in more detail below.

The FocusMap is the currently active data frame.

The ActiveView property provides an IActiveView interface, which links the document data to the current screen display of that data. It is especially useful for controlling the view extent. Panning or zooming can be accomplished by simply setting the view extent to the desired document area covered by the view.

The IActiveView interface reported by MxDocument may refer to either a data view (as a Map object) or page layout view (PageLayout object), depending on the current application state. You can resolve this ambiguity by querying the active view object for IMap or IPageLayout. In Visual Basic, this can be done using the TypeOf keyword:

```
' Define interface pointer
Dim pActiveView as IActiveView
' Get active view of document
Set pActiveView = pMxDoc.ActiveView
' Test the view object type
If Typeof pActiveView Is IMap Then
' It's a Map object
Else
' It's a PageLayout object
End If
```

The StyleGallery maintains the collection of styles referenced by the current document.

When using the VB Editor within ArcMap, the predefined variable ThisDocument is the IDocument interface to an MxDocument object.

The AppDisplay object presents a map view on the user's screen.

It handles basic drawing and screen control functions.

The DisplayTransformation property gives you access to the object that does coordinate transformations between map and screen device units for the current view.

Other application-related objects

PageLayout represents a view that shows how the map document will appear as printed output. It holds the ruler settings and snap guides used by the view and is the source for printer device settings and sheet size.

PageLayout's GraphicsContainer property lists the map document contents as graphical objects. These include MapFrame, MapSurroundFrame, and graphic element objects used for symbology and text.

DataWindow class covers three utility window objects. MapInsetWindow (magnifier) and OverviewWindow (data overview) are normally created in response to a command selection from the main menu View dropdown. The TableWindow (layer attribute grid) appears in the feature layer context menu (right-click on a layer name) as "Open Attribute Table".

There is no explicit object property that points to these windows when they are active. They all use the main application window as their parent and so are automatically destroyed when it closes.

Map components

A map document is organized as a hierarchy of maps, layers, and elements. MxDocument.Maps is the collection of all maps in the current ArcMap document. MxDocument.FocusMap is the map that is currently selected for user interaction.

A Map object corresponds to a data frame entry in ArcMap's Table of Contents window. It maintains a collection of map layers

(e.g., geodatabase features) and map surrounds (e.g., legends and scale bars).

Map.Name is the data frame name.

Individual map layers may be accessed via Layer() and an index value or by Layers() (plural) and the UID of a layer type-specific interface.

The BasicGraphicsLayer contains "basic graphics"—that is, graphic elements not directly described in a database. These include features that have been converted to graphics and elements added by drawing tools.

MapSurround() provides the list of map surround objects.

Scale and SpatialReference are metric properties common to all layers of a given map.

Each map has its own list of bookmarks, available through the IMapBookmarks interface. Bookmarks managed through the main menu options are of the AOIBookmark type (AOI = "area of interest").

Map layers are represented by various types of layer objects according to the type of data they present.

A FeatureLayer presents geodata-defined map elements (features) stored as feature class data in a geodatabase.

An FDOGraphicsLayer (FDO = "feature data object") presents annotation feature class data. Annotation features are graphical elements used to annotate members of a feature layer. FDOGraphicsLayer data is also stored in a geodatabase.

Map uses a CompositeGraphicsLayer for its BasicGraphicsLayer property and a CoverageAnnotationLayer for display of ArcInfo coverage files.

RasterLayer and TinLayer present raster and TIN data, respectively.

A GroupLayer treats multiple layers as a single unit.

A given map may contain layers of different types. All layer objects implement the ILayer interface, and this is what is returned by Map's layer selection functions. To determine the exact layer type, you need to try querying the object for type-specific interfaces. For example, if the layer object supports the IFeatureLayer interface, then you know it is a FeatureLayer object. In Visual Basic, this might be coded as follows:

```
Dim pLayer as ILayer
Set pLayer = pMap.Layer(0)
' (pMap points to Map object)
If Typeof pLayer Is IFeatureLayer Then
   ' pLayer is a FeatureLayer object
End If
```

GraphicElement objects are used for the display of nonfeature data (a FeatureLayer displays itself using a feature renderer acting on each record of the layer dataset). Graphic elements include text, primitive geometric shapes, and pictures. (Graphs and reports are stored as EmfPictureElements.)

The MapSurround class includes legends, scale bars, and North arrows.

Objects derived from MapGrid, MapGridBorder, and GridLabel provide support for map grids. Members of the NumberFormat class assist in grid labeling with a variety of numeric display format options.

FrameElements serve as graphical containers for other objects. In addition to providing backgrounds and borders, they perform other functions according to their type:

A MapFrame houses a Map object. It stores map grids, locator rectangles, and clipping parameters.

A MapSurroundFrame houses a MapSurround object.

Use an OleFrame to embed an OLE object into a map document.

Adding a layer to a map without user intervention

Users routinely add layers during the course of an ArcMap session by selecting the Add Data command. On the other hand, they may work with templates that already have data loaded; however, they may have requirements to provide data for a map without user intervention or the browser. An example of this might be a "kiosk" application, where the data might be loaded by some means other than directly choosing the data from the database. The two VBA examples that follow show how to add data from a shapefile and a PersonalSDE (Access) database. Note that the examples accept the default symbology for the layer.

How To

To add a layer derived from a shapefile to a map, your code should do the following:

1. First you'll need to get the workspace that contains the feature class. Using a WorkspaceFactory, create a FeatureWorkspace for ▶

```
Sub AddShapefileData()

    Dim pWF As IWorkspaceFactory
    Set pWF = New ShapefileWorkspaceFactory
    Dim pFWS As IFeatureWorkspace
    Set pFWS = pWF.OpenFromFile("d:\Data\Shapefiles\USA", 0)    ❶

    Dim pFClass As IFeatureClass
    Set pFClass = pFWS.OpenFeatureClass("States")    ❷

    Dim pFLayer As IFeatureLayer
    Set pFLayer = New FeatureLayer

    Set pFLayer.FeatureClass = pFClass    ❸

    Dim pDataset As IDataset
    Set pDataset = pFClass    ❹
    pFLayer.Name = pDataset.Name

    Dim pDoc As IMxDocument
    Set pDoc = ThisDocument
    pDoc.AddLayer pFLayer    ❺

End Sub
```

the shapefile. Provide the name of the folder on disk that contains the data as the parameter.

2. Create a FeatureClass. Specify the name of the shapefile as the feature class.

3. Establish a new Feature Layer to add to the map.

4. Set the name for the layer. QueryInterface to IDataset to get the name.

5. Add the layer to the document.

How To

To add a layer derived from a Personal geodatabase (Access) database to a map, your code should follow the same procedures as in the previous example except:

1. Use an AccessWorkspaceFactory. Provide the full pathname of the database that contains the data as the parameter.

2. Specify the name of the Table as the feature class.

```
Public Sub AddAccessData()

    Dim pWF As IWorkspaceFactory
    Set pWF = New AccessWorkspaceFactory
    Dim pFWS As IFeatureWorkspace
    Set pFWS = pWF.OpenFromFile("D:\data\usa.mdb", 0)    1

    Dim pFClass As IFeatureClass
    Set pFClass = pFWS.OpenFeatureClass("States")    2

    Dim pFLayer As IFeatureLayer
    Set pFLayer = New FeatureLayer

    Set pFLayer.FeatureClass = pFClass

    Dim pDataset As IDataset
    Set pDataset = pFClass
    pFLayer.Name = pDataset.Name

    Dim pDoc As IMxDocument
    Set pDoc = ThisDocument
    pDoc.AddLayer pFLayer

End Sub
```

Creating your own startup dialog

When ArcMap starts, a splash screen appears followed by a startup dialog. You can create your own version of this dialog to provide similar functionality, provide a login/password dialog, or supply functionality that your application requires prior to the display of the ArcMap application.

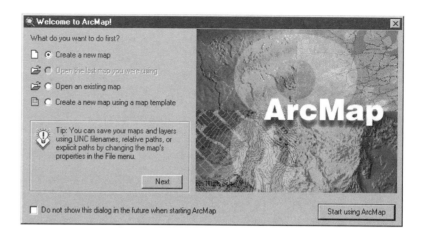

The ArcMap startup dialog appears after the initial splash screen.

In order to create a new startup dialog, you should write code to do the following:

1. Create a class that will allow you to provide a means to show a form that will serve as the dialog. In this class, you'll implement the methods of the IStartupDialog interface.

2. In the DoModal method display a form of your own design, making certain that its display style is modal.

3. Set the appropriate registry entries to indicate the name of the fully qualified class name or programmatic ID associated with the ActiveX DLL you've written and whether or not to display the dialog. This step must be performed in a setup program or manually.

```
Implements IStartupDialog  ❶
Option Explicit

Private Sub IStartupDialog_DoModal()  ❷
    frmLogin.Show vbModal
End Sub

Private Property Get IStartupDialog_FilePath() As String
    IStartupDialog_FilePath = ""
End Property
```

❸

HKEY_CURRENT_USER\Software\ESRI\ArcMap\Settings\ShowStartup is set to 1 to display the dialog. 0 to not display the dialog. The Show startup dialog flag checkbox in the Application tab of the Options dialog also controls this setting.

HKEY_CURRENT_USER\Software\ESRI\ArcMap\Settings\StartupProgID is the programmatic ID. The programmatic ID is visible in the General tab of the Options dialog.

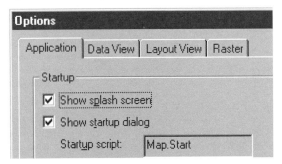

The Display object model

The objects in the Display object model perform basic functions for displaying map symbology, showing graphical editing feedback markers, performing coordinate transformations, and controlling the screen display.

Symbols

Objects derived from Symbol specify symbol attributes such as color, style, and orientation. A symbol object by itself is not sufficient to display the shape it describes. It must be combined with geometry information (for symbol location) within a graphic element object in order to be displayable. The same symbol object may be used to set the attributes for more than one symbol instance.

There are four general classes derived from Symbol:

- A MarkerSymbol is characterized by having its location described as a point.

- A LineSymbol may follow a curve as well as a straight line.

- A FillSymbol is a closed, two-dimensional figure whose interior may be filled with patterns (line or marker), colors (solid or gradient), or bitmaps.

- A TextSymbol contains the symbol's text string, does character formatting, and controls the text background.

TextSymbol allows setting the orientation of its text according to the geometry type assigned to it.

If a Point geometry is used, the text is displayed starting at the given point location and following a baseline direction per the Angle property.

If a curve geometry is used (e.g., Polyline, EllipticArc, Ring, BezierCurve), the text baseline will follow the curve. TextPath objects are created by TextSymbol for this purpose.

If an Envelope geometry is used, the text will be drawn in the specified envelope rectangle.

Marker, line, and fill symbol classes also each have a multilayer type to allow creating compound symbols built from multiple layers of simple symbols.

Feature renderers

A feature renderer is responsible for displaying feature record data from a geodatabase. No permanent graphic objects are created in a document representing feature data. The renderer creates symbology 'on the fly' as it makes a pass through a feature class's recordset.

Renderers allow changing the appearance of a feature based on attributes of the record data. The renderer object types parallel the options listed in the Show window of the Symbology tab of the layer properties property sheet.

The SimpleRenderer draws with a fixed set of attributes that are independent of the data.

The ClassBreaksRenderer can present differing representations according to a list of data expression value ranges (classes). Classify objects are used in rendering setup dialogs to calculate the value range divisions (class breaks).

The ProportionalSymbolRenderer, UniqueValueRenderer, and BiUniqueValueRenderer also control the look of a feature according to a specified evaluation of record data.

The ScaleDependentRenderer adds additional renderering control based on the display scale.

Display feedback and selection tracking

DisplayFeedback objects display the simple temporary shapes that are generally used during mouse dragging operations to show relocation or resizing. These objects do not handle mouse messages themselves. They just facilitate showing and moving a graphic marker that is appropriate for a particular geometry type.

A SelectionTracker also provides display feedback, but it includes methods for responding to mouse and keyboard events. This facilitates implementing tracking functions in a more convenient and standard way thoughout the application.

A RubberBand object is a more self-contained tracker that gets its own mouse and keyboard messages internally.

Color

Color-derived objects are used for specifying color values used by other objects such as symbols. Several types of color objects exist to allow defining the color according to different color models (RGB, HLS, CIELAB, grayscale, etc.).

A ColorRamp is a list of color values commonly used by a feature render for data-dependent feature display. Color ramps differ according to how the list colors are determined. They can be explicitly set (PresetColorRamp), calculated (AlgorithmicColorRamp), or chosen at random (RandomColorRamp).

The CieLabConversion object encapsulates conversion and attribute functions for colors expressed in the CIELAB model.

Display

ScreenDisplay contains basic application view window functions and attributes. It also maintains the display cache, which is a collection of memory-based bitmaps. Maps are not drawn directly to the view window, but to one of these bitmaps. The window is updated from the bitmap at the end of the drawing operation. This technique improves the performance of screen updates and view panning.

StartDrawing and FinishDrawing calls are used to bracket most map drawing actions. These functions define the cache bitmap on which the drawing will take place. You can also force drawing directly to the view window by giving StartDrawing a cache ID parameter value of esriNoScreenCache (= -1).

PanStart, PanMoveTo, and PanStop allow panning the current view using mouse position coordinates.

DisplayTransformation (a property of ScreenDisplay) translates point coordinates between map units and output device units (e.g., pixels) according to the spatial reference and scale of the map that is currently active.

Creating a unique value renderer

In the Symbology panel of the Properties dialog, users can select from a variety of renderers. One of these renderers symbolizes features based on unique values the features share. The dialog makes it possible to create this type of symbolization easily—and with no code; nevertheless, it may prove instructive to see the techniques used to create a UniqueValueRenderer as a precursor to creating a custom renderer. The following example code assumes that the sample 'STATES' layer is in the map and that the field used to render is the 'SUB_REGION' field.

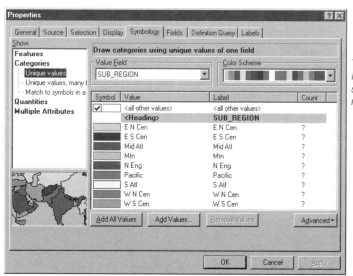

The Symbology panel of the Properties dialog presents various symbolization options, resulting in a map as illustrated below.

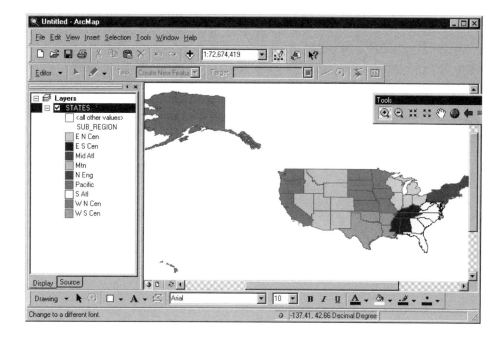

If you want to write your own UniqueValueRenderer, your code should do the following:

1. Create a color ramp and set its size to the number of features.

2. Create a color enumeration for retrieving a sequence of colors.

3. Create a new unique value renderer.

4. Loop through the features and add a value to the renderer for each feature.

5. Associate the renderer with the layer, update the TOC and refresh the active view.

```
Public Sub SetUniqueValue()
    Dim pMxDoc As IMxDocument
    Dim pFLayer As IGeoFeatureLayer
    Dim pFClass As IFeatureClass
    Dim pFeature As IFeature
    Dim pFCursor As IFeatureCursor
    Dim pUVRenderer As IUniqueValueRenderer
    Dim pColorEnum As IEnumColors
    Dim pCRamp As IColorRamp
    Dim pSym As ISimpleFillSymbol

    Set pMxDoc = Application.Document
    Set pFLayer = pMxDoc.ActiveView.FocusMap.Layer(0)
    Set pFClass = pFLayer.FeatureClass
    Set pFCursor = pFClass.Search(Nothing, False)
    Set pFeature = pFCursor.NextFeature

    ' Create a color ramp and set its size to the number of features ❶
    Set pCRamp = New RandomColorRamp
    pCRamp.Size = pFClass.FeatureCount(Nothing)
    pCRamp.CreateRamp True

    'Create a color enumeration for retrieving a sequence of colors ❷
    Set pColorEnum = pCRamp.Colors

    'Create a new unique value renderer    ❸
    Set pUVRenderer = New UniqueValueRenderer
    pUVRenderer.FieldCount = 1
    pUVRenderer.Field(0) = "SUB_REGION"
```

```
' Loop through the features and add a value to the renderer  ④
' for each feature
Do Until pFeature Is Nothing
   Set pSym = New SimpleFillSymbol
   pSym.Color = pColorEnum.Next
   pUVRenderer.AddValue _
   pFeature.Value(pFClass.FindField("SUB_REGION")), _
   "Sub_Region", pSym
   Set pFeature = pFCursor.NextFeature
Loop

' Associate the renderer with the layer, update the TOC,  ⑤
' and refresh the active view
Set pFLayer.Renderer = pUVRenderer
pMxDoc.UpdateContents
pMxDoc.ActiveView.Refresh
End Sub
```

Working with the color dialogs

In the course of your work, you may need to invoke a color dialog to set a color value. You may have seen one of the dialogs in action in the applications. The object model makes several kinds of dialogs available as illustrated here.

Each dialog sets a Color property that can then be assigned as your application requires. If the user selects a color, the dialog returns True; if the user clicks Cancel or otherwise quits the dialog without making a selection, the dialog returns False.

Color Browser

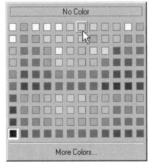

Color Palette

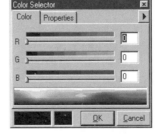

Color Selector

This VBA example assumes that the FocusMap has a layer with polygon features as its topmost layer. For example purposes only, the MxDocument initializes a UIComboBoxControl with a brief instruction and the names of the three color selection dialogs.

If your code is similar to the example, when the user chooses a color selection method, it should do the following:

1. Create a color selection object.

2. Display the selected dialog. In all likelihood, your code will display a specific dialog only.

3. Given the user's selection, return the Color.

4. Use the color as desired.

```vba
Private Function MxDocument_OpenDocument() As Boolean
   With UIComboBoxControl1
      .AddItem "<Choose how to pick layer color>"
      .AddItem "ColorBrowser"
      .AddItem "ColorPalette"
      .AddItem "ColorSelector"
      .ListIndex = 0
   End With
End Function


Private Sub UIComboBoxControl1_SelectionChange(ByVal newIndex As Long)
   Dim pdoc As IMxDocument
   Dim pMap As IMap
   Dim pFeatureLayer As IGeoFeatureLayer

   Set pdoc = Application.Document
   Set pMap = pdoc.FocusMap
   If TypeOf pMap.Layer(0) Is IFeatureLayer Then
      Set pFeatureLayer = pMap.Layer(0)
      If pFeatureLayer.FeatureClass.ShapeType <> esriGeometryPolygon Then
        Exit Sub
      End If
   Else
      Exit Sub
   End If

   Dim pSimpleRenderer As ISimpleRenderer
   Dim pFeatureRenderer As IFeatureRenderer

   Dim pSimpleFillsymbol As ISimpleFillSymbol
   Dim pRGBColor As IRgbColor
```

```
Set pSimpleRenderer = New SimpleRenderer
Set pSimpleFillsymbol = New SimpleFillSymbol
Set pRGBColor = New RgbColor

Select Case newIndex
  Case 0
    Exit Sub
  Case 1
    Dim pColorBrowser As IColorBrowser
    Set pColorBrowser = New ColorBrowser           ❶
    pColorBrowser.Color = pRGBColor

    If pColorBrowser.DoModal(Application.hWnd) Then ❷
      Set pRGBColor = pColorBrowser.Color           ❸
    Else
      Exit Sub
    End If
  Case 2
    Dim pColorPalette As IColorPalette
    Set pColorPalette = New ColorPalette            ❶
    Dim pRect As tagRECT
    pRect.bottom = 300
    pRect.Left = 500
    pRect.Right = 0
    pRect.top = 0

    If pColorPalette.TrackPopupMenu(pRect, pRGBColor, False) Then  ❷
      Set pRGBColor = pColorPalette.Color           ❸
    Else
      Exit Sub
    End If
```

```
    Case 3
      Dim pColorSelector As IColorSelector    ①
      Set pColorSelector = New ColorSelector
      pColorSelector.Color = pRGBColor

      If pColorSelector.DoModal(Application.hWnd) Then    ②
        Set pRGBColor = pColorSelector.Color              ③
      Else
        Exit Sub
      End If
  End Select

  pSimpleFillsymbol.Color = pRGBColor    ④
  pSimpleFillsymbol.Style = esriSFSSolid

  Set pSimpleRenderer.Symbol = pSimpleFillsymbol

  Set pFeatureLayer.Renderer = pSimpleRenderer

  pdoc.ActiveView.Refresh
  pdoc.UpdateContents
  UIComboBoxControl1.ListIndex = 0
End Sub
```

The ArcMap Editor object model

The ArcMap Editor is an end-user product that provides a common editing environment for features stored in all types of vector geographic datasets: geodatabases, coverages, and shapefiles. The Editor primarily consists of tools for editing and maintaining GIS databases; these tools offer the following:

- Advanced feature entry and modification
- Geometric operators and CAD-like editing
- Multilayer feature snapping
- Rule-based editing
- Undo/Redo capabilities
- Multiuse editing and versioning

The Editor also contains an accessible underlying framework or object model. The object model is a set of COM components that are used to create the Editor tools. Developers can use these objects to create new custom tools. "Tools" describes all of the components that perform editing; there are many distinctions.

Edit operations typically occur through one of four methods: commands, tools, tasks, and edit event notifications. Commands perform edits without the user interacting with the mouse. For example, the Buffer command creates new features by buffering the selected features—aside from entering the buffer distance, the command does not require any user interaction. Tools require user interaction. For example, the Split tool requires the user to specify the point where the split will occur. Edit tasks require input geometry to perform their edits. A good example is the Reshape task, which uses sketch geometry created by the user to modify a selected feature's shape. Edit events are notifications that occur during an edit session, and edit event listeners are any objects that respond to the events.

Editor components

Editor commands

The Editor uses commands for all operations that do not require user interaction with the display. Examples of commands include the Buffer, Intersect, and Union commands. Commands may ask for keyboard input, but none of them require the user to interact with the display. Most commands reside on the Editor pulldown menu.

All commands implement the ICommand interface. For more details on creating a custom command, see Chapter 5, 'Working with the Customization Framework'. An example of a custom command that a developer might create is a Difference command. A command such as this could create new features based on the collective geometry of two selected features.

Editor tools

The Editor uses tools for all operations that require the user to interact with the display. The Sketch tool, the Rotate tool, and the Split tool are all examples of Editor tools. All of these tools expect and react to the user clicking on the map. Tools generally reside directly on the Editor toolbar.

All tools implement the ITool and ICommand interfaces. For more details on creating a custom tool, see Chapter 5. An example of a custom tool that might be created and added to the Editor toolbar is a Fillet tool. A Fillet tool would ask the user to select two segments and then create a fillet line between them based on a radius value.

Edit tasks

For edit operations that require input geometry, the Editor uses edit tasks. Edit tasks are command-like components that acquire the geometry stored in a user-created edit sketch and perform a specific operation with it. For example, the Reshape task uses the geometry of an edit sketch a user digitizes on the map to alter the shape of a selected feature. The edit tasks are managed as a collection, and there can only be one current task. The current task is set with the IEditor::CurrentTask property.

All edit tasks implement the IEditTask interface and are registered in the Edit Tasks component category. An example of a custom edit task might be a Measure task that simply reports the length of an edit sketch. The benefit of such a task would be that the user could digitize a line using all of the already available CAD-like sketch tools. All edit tasks appear in the Current Task dropdown list on the Editor toolbar.

Edit events

Edit events are specific notifications that occur during editing. Edit event notifications are completely hidden from the user— they have no interaction or knowledge of them. Edit event listeners are objects such as a command that detect and perform an edit operation whenever a specific edit event occurs. For example, a specific edit event is fired each time a new feature is created, and a custom object could perform feature validation after receiving this notification.

Editor concepts

Edit session

All editing takes place within the confines of an edit session. Only one workspace is editable at a time. All of the layers that have been added to a map and belong to the same workspace are editable simultaneously.

Edit sketch

The Editor facilitates geometric construction and modification by managing a temporary staging area for coordinates that is called the edit sketch. The edit sketch is a pure geometry that is used as input for completion of a specific task. The sketch geometry may be a single point, a multipoint, a polyline, or a polygon. The dimensionality of the sketch is typically determined by the current edit task. The edit sketch is owned by the Editor and accessed via the IEditSketch interface. Access to the edit sketch geometry is through the IEditSketch::Geometry property.

When the edit sketch is finished, the current editing task takes the geometry stored in the edit sketch and performs a specific operation with it. For example, completing the sketch of a building outline when the current task is set to Create New Feature and the target layer is set to the Buildings feature class will create a new Building feature.

All of the available sketch tools can be used together to create an edit sketch. For example, the Intersection tool and the Distance-Distance tool can be used interchangeably to create a single edit sketch. A custom sketch tool is another example of a custom tool that can be created and added to the Editor toolbar.

The edit sketch has its own context menu that aids in the manipulation of the edit sketch geometry. Commands that appear on this menu include Move, Move To, Insert, and Delete. Right-clicking on top of any part of the edit sketch invokes the edit sketch context menu no matter what the active tool is. Custom commands can be added to the edit sketch context menu through the Customize dialog.

Sketch operations

All editing tools and commands that create or modify the geometry of an edit sketch use a sketch operation to provide undo/redo capabilities. Sketch operations add the edit to the undo/redo operation stack. For example, the Edit tool is able to move edit sketch vertices and does so using sketch operations so that each action is undoable. Always use sketch operations when writing a custom tool or command that alters the edit sketch's geometry. Code that modifies the edit sketch should be placed between calls to ISketchOperation::Start and ISketchOperation::Finish.

Edit operations

All commands, tools, and edit tasks use edit operations to make all edits undoable. Edit operations are very similar to sketch operations except that these are operations on existing features instead of the edit sketch. For example, if a feature is moved with the Edit tool, the operation can be undone and redone.

Edit operations are created in the IEditor interface by placing the relevant code between calls to IEditor::StartOperation and IEditor::StopOperation.

Snap agents

The Editor also maintains a snapping environment that contains several snapping agents used for ensuring the requisite connectivity when modifying and creating features. For example, the sketch tools use snap agents to precisely position points added to the edit sketch such as the corner of a building.

All snap agents implement the ISnapAgent interface and are registered in the Editor Snap Agents component category. A specific class of snap agent is the feature snap agent. The sketch tools and other editing tools use feature snap agents to find features to snap to. The Editor automatically instantiates a feature snap agent for each editable feature class the first time the snapping window is opened. The other snap agents such as Snap Perpendicular are instantiated when they are clicked on in the

snapping window. The snapping properties such as snap tolerance, snap tolerance units (map or pixel), and hittype are managed by the ISnapEnvironment interface on the Editor object.

You can perform snapping by calling the ISnapEnvironment::SnapPoint method and passing it an IPoint. For example, the sketch tools get the current mouse location, convert it to an IPoint, and call SnapPoint passing in the IPoint. SnapPoint in turn calls each snap agent's ISnapAgent::Snap method until one of them returns True. True indicates that the snap agent has found a new point that meets its unique snapping criteria. The coordinates of the point are modified to reflect that of the new point location.

Feature snap agents use feature caches to create a small selected set of features in memory. The feature snap agents track the current mouse location and continually reinitialize a feature cache and fill it with the features that reside near this point. The snap agents then cycle through all of the features in a cache and check to see if any of them are within the Editor's snap tolerance.

Editor extensions

Just as the Editor is an extension to ArcMap, the Editor also has its own extensions. The Editor ships with three extensions: the Digitizer extension, the Topology Editor extension, and the Conflict Resolution extension. All Editor extensions implement the IExtension interface and are registered in the ESRI Edit Extensions component category. When an edit session begins, each Editor extension is activated; when editing is complete, each Editor extension is deactivated.

Custom Editor extensions can be created and added to the Editor. For example, a developer may choose to create a custom extension that controls feature validation throughout an edit session. Such an extension might listen for the edit events

OnCreateFeature and OnChangeFeature and perform validation when it detects these events.

Feature inspectors

The Attributes dialog button on the Editor toolbar activates the Editor's attributes dialog. The Attributes dialog has two panels. The left panel of the dialog contains the features from the map that have been selected and the names of the feature classes they belong to. The right panel contains a feature inspector. The default feature inspector lists and allows users to edit all of the attributes of a selected feature. Users can replace this inspector with their own customized feature inspector. For example, you may want to create a custom feature inspector that displays a bitmap whenever a feature belonging to a specific feature class is selected.

Only one feature inspector can be active for each feature class. When you create a custom feature inspector, you specify the specific feature classes that will use it. Selecting a feature in the left panel of the Attributes dialog activates the associated feature inspector in the right panel.

Creating a custom edit task

ArcMap's Editing toolbar has a dropdown list of tasks that can be used to take a geometry and perform some action with it. Each edit task performs a different operation with this geometry. For example, the CreateNewFeature edit task takes the edit sketch and stores it as a new feature. The Reshape Feature edit task uses the edit sketch to reshape a selected feature. You can add custom tasks to this list to meet the demands of your own application.

While your application may require a far more sophisticated operation on a geometry, you'll see the implementation that's required for all editing tasks in the simple measuring tool that's created by the code that follows. Written in Visual Basic, the code can be compiled to create an ActiveX DLL.

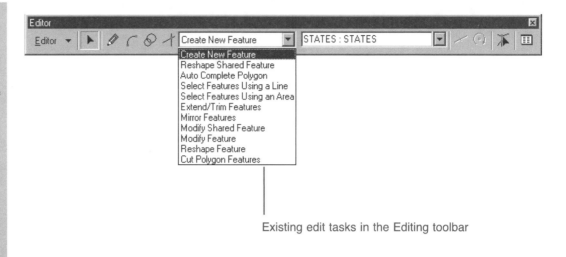

Existing edit tasks in the Editing toolbar

In order to create a new edit task, you should write code to do the following:

1. Create a class that will allow you to provide a means to manipulate the geometry. In this class, you'll implement the methods of the IEditTask interface.

2. Get the geometry from the Editor and specify its type. In order to make the measurement tool flexible, the edit sketch will be a polyline.

3. Give the task a name. This will be the text that appears in the Editing toolbar's dropdown list of edit tasks.

4. Perform the operation on the geometry; in this case, report the length of the polyline.

```
Option Explicit

Implements IEditTask    'Create a new Edit Task
Private m_pEdSketch As IEditSketch    'Make use of the EditSketch

Private Sub IEditTask_Activate(ByVal Editor As esriCore.IEditor, ByVal
oldTask As esriCore.IEditTask)
    'Query Interface to set the EditSketch object from the Editor interface
    Set m_pEdSketch = Editor
    'This task uses a Polyline geometry
    m_pEdSketch.GeometryType = esriGeometryPolyline
End Sub

Private Sub IEditTask_Deactivate()
    'Nothing needed in the Deactivate event, but
    'this is the method called when the task completes
    'use it for clean up
End Sub

Private Property Get IEditTask_Name() As String
    'Give the task a name - appears in the dropdown list
    IEditTask_Name = "Measure Length"
End Property

Private Sub IEditTask_OnDeleteSketch()
    'Nothing needed in the OnDeleteSketch event
End Sub
```

```
Private Sub IEditTask_OnFinishSketch()
  Dim pMeasureLine As Ipolyline 'the geometry that performs the measure
  Dim pLocalEditor As IEditor 'Declare a local version of the Editor
  'Query Interface to get back an Editor object
  Set pLocalEditor = m_pEdSketch
  'The measuring geometry is the geometry from
  Set pMeasureLine = m_pEdSketch.Geometry
  MsgBox "Length:" & Chr(13) & Format(pMeasureLine.Length, "0.00000"),  _
vbInformation
End Sub
```

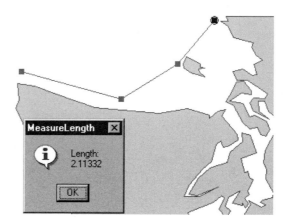

Creating a custom snap agent

To provide more precision in the editing process, the ArcMap Editor provides a variety of snapping agents. You can create custom snap agents by implementing ISnapAgent. Tools that work with snapping typically call ISnapEnvironment's SnapPoint method every time the mouse moves. SnapPoint in turn calls each snap agent's Snap method in succession until one of them returns true. True means a new point has been found that meets the qualifications set within a particular snap agent's Snap method. This snap agent snaps to the center of polygons using the Editor's current snap tolerance. The snap agent has a special feature class property that enables you to set the polygon feature class you want to snap to.

```
Option Explicit

Implements ISnapAgent          (1)
Implements IPersistVariant

Private m_FeatureCache As IFeatureCache
Private m_bSetNewFeatureCache As Boolean
Private m_FeatureClass As IFeatureClass
Private m_CacheFilled As Boolean

Private Property Get IPersistVariant_ID() As esriCore.IUID
   Dim pID As New UID
   pID = "CenterSnap.clsCenterSnap"     (2)
   Set IPersistVariant_ID = pID
End Property

Private Sub IPersistVariant_Load(ByVal stream As esriCore.IVariantStream)
End Sub

Private Sub IPersistVariant_Save(ByVal stream As esriCore.IVariantStream)
End Sub

Private Property Get ISnapAgent_Name() As String
   ISnapAgent_Name = "Center Snap"
End Property                          (3)
```

In order to create a snap agent, you should write code to do the following:

1. Create a class that will allow you to provide a means to perform the snapping operation. In this class, you'll implement the methods of the ISnapAgent interface.

2. Provide an ID for the snap agent that will be created.

3. Give the task a name. This will be the text that appears in the Snapping Environment dialog.

4. Implement the Snap method that's unique to the snap agent.

```vb
Private Function ISnapAgent_Snap(ByVal geom As esriCore.IGeometry, ByVal ④
point As esriCore.IPoint, ByVal tolerance As Double) As Boolean

Dim Index As Integer, Count As Integer
Dim PartCount As Integer, PartIndex As Integer
Dim Dist As Double, minDist As Double
Dim pFeature As IFeature
Dim pArea As IArea
Dim pProximity As IProximityOperator
Dim pGeoCollection As IGeometryCollection
Dim x As Double, y As Double

Set pProximity = point
minDist = tolerance * 10

'Check if a feature cache has been created
If Not m_bSetNewFeatureCache Then
  SetNewFeatureCache
End If

'Check if a FeatureClass is present
If m_FeatureClass is Nothing Then
  ISnapAgent_Snap = False
  Exit Function
End If

'Make sure the feature class has Polygons
If Not m_FeatureClass.ShapeType = esriGeometryPolygon Then
  ISnapAgent_Snap = False
  Exit Function
End If
```

```
'Fill the New Cache with the geometries
If Not m_CacheFilled Then
  FillCache m_FeatureClass, point, 500
  m_CacheFilled = True
End If

'If the point isn't within the cache call FillCache again
If Not m_FeatureCache.Contains(point) Then
  FillCache m_FeatureClass, point, tolerance * 10
End If

'Loop through all of the features and their parts
For Count = 0 To m_FeatureCache.Count - 1
  Set pFeature = m_FeatureCache.Feature(Count)
  Set pGeoCollection = pFeature.Shape
  For PartCount = 0 To pGeoCollection.GeometryCount - 1
    Set pArea = pGeoCollection.Geometry(PartCount)
    Dist = pProximity.ReturnDistance(pArea.LabelPoint)
    If Dist < minDist Then
      Index = Count
      minDist = Dist
      PartIndex = PartCount
    End If
  Next PartCount
Next Count

'Make sure minDist is within the search tolerance
If minDist >= tolerance Then
  ISnapAgent_Snap = False
  Exit Function
End If
```

```
'Retrieve the feature and its part again
Set pFeature = m_FeatureCache.Feature(Index)
Set pGeoCollection = pFeature.Shape
Set pArea = pGeoCollection.Geometry(PartIndex)
'Since point was passed in ByValue, we have to modify its values instead
'of giving it a new address
pArea.LabelPoint.QueryCoords x, y
point.PutCoords x, y

ISnapAgent_Snap = True

End Function


Public Property Let FeatureClass(ByRef FeatClass As IFeatureClass)
  'Public so the user can set and read the FeatureClass to constrain on
  Set m_FeatureClass = FeatClass
End Property


Public Property Get FeatureClass() As IFeatureClass
  Set FeatureClass = m_FeatureClass
End Property


Private Sub FillCache(FClass As IFeatureClass, pPoint As IPoint, Distance As
Double)
  m_FeatureCache.Initialize pPoint, Distance
  m_FeatureCache.AddFeatures FClass
End Sub
```

Tip

When you're done

1. Compile the code that represents the class.

2. Run Categories.exe in the installation's bin folder and add CenterSnap to ESRI Snap Agents.

3. In ArcMap, start an edit session with at least one polygon layer loaded.

4. In VBE, add the macro SetMySnapAgentFClass.

5. In the VBE Tools menu select References and then add 'CenterSnap'.

6. Close VBE and return to your editing session.

7. In the Editor menu, select Snapping. The custom snap agent should appear in the bottom half of the window. Click it on.

8. Set the Editor's current layer to the polygon layer you want to snap to and then run the adjacent macro. This script sets the feature class to snap to.

9. Select the Editor's sketch tool.

```
Private Sub SetNewFeatureCache()
  Set m_FeatureCache = New FeatureCache
  m_bSetNewFeatureCache = True
End Sub



Public Sub SetMySnapAgentFClass()
  On Error Resume Next
  Dim pApp As IApplication
  Dim pEditor As IEditor
  Dim pSnapAgent As ISnapAgent
  Dim pSnapEnv As ISnapEnvironment
  Dim pEditLayers As IEditLayers
  Dim pMySnapAgent As CenterSnap.clsCenterSnap
  Dim pUID As New UID
  Dim Count As Integer

  pUID = "esriCore.Editor"
  Set pApp = Application
  Set pEditor = pApp.FindExtensionByCLSID(pUID)
  Set pEditLayers = pEditor 'QI
  Set pSnapEnv = pEditor 'QI
  'Find custom snap agent and set is featureclass property
  For Count = 0 To pSnapEnv.SnapAgentCount - 1
    Set pSnapAgent = pSnapEnv.SnapAgent(Count)
    If pSnapAgent.Name = "Center Snap" Then
     Set pMySnapAgent = pSnapAgent
     pMySnapAgent.FeatureClass = pEditLayers.CurrentLayer.FeatureClass
    End If
  Next Count
End Sub
```

Mapping commands and tools to digitizer buttons

If there are ArcMap commands that you use more than others when digitizing, it may be useful to map these commands to the digitizer puck. This lets you control your ArcMap session directly from the digitizing board rather than from the workstation. For example, when digitizing a new line feature that contains a true curve segment, it is quicker to switch tools (from the Sketch Tool to the ArcTool) directly from the puck.

Mapping commands to digitizer buttons requires the IDigitizerButtons interface (part of the ArcMap Editor's digitizer extension). The following code demonstrates how to get a handle to the digitizer extension and shows how to map specific ArcMap commands and tools to specific digitizer buttons.

Tip

Mouse-related events
All mouse-related events must be set in the digitizer control panel. For this example, you should set 'Left Click', 'Left Drag', and 'Left Double-Click' to 0, 1, and 2, respectively. Make sure buttons 3, 4, 5, 6, 8, and 9 are set to none.

```
Public Sub MapDigitizerBtns()
  Dim pApp As IApplication
  Dim pEditor As IEditor
  Dim pDigitizerBnts As IDigitizerButtons
  Dim pID As New UID
  Set pApp = MxApplication
  pID = "esriCore.Editor"
  'Get a handle to ArcMap's editor extension
  Set pEditor = pApp.FindExtensionByCLSID(pID)  ①
  'Get a handle to the editor's digitizer extension
  pID = "esriCore.DigitizerExtension"  ②
  Set pDigitizerBnts = pEditor.FindExtension(pID)
  'Set button 3  to execute the FinishSketch command
  pID = "esriCore.FinishSketchCommand"
  pDigitizerBnts.Button(3) = pID  ③
  'Set buttons 4, 5, and 6 to switch to the specified tool
  pID = "esriCore.EditTool"
  pDigitizerBnts.Button(4) = pID
  pID = "esriCore.SketchTool"
  pDigitizerBnts.Button(5) = pID
  pID = "esriCore.ArcTool"
  pDigitizerBnts.Button(6) = pID
  'Set button 8 to execute the ZoomIn fixed command
  pID = "esriCore.ZoomInFixedCommand"
  pDigitizerBnts.Button(8) = pID
  'Set button 9 to execute the ZoomOut fixed command
  pID = "esriCore.ZoomOutFixedCommand"
  pDigitizerBnts.Button(9) = pID
End Sub
```

To map commands to the digitizer buttons, you should write code to do the following:

1. Get a handle to ArcMap's Editor extension.

2. Get a handle to the Editor's digitizer extension.

3. Set individual buttons on the digitizer to execute a specific command or switch to a specific tool.

Tip

When you're done

Start an ArcMap edit session, switch to the Visual Basic Editor and execute the code. Pressing button 5 on the digitizer puck will now select the Sketch tool—you may have to click once to activate the puck. Pressing button 4 will switch you to the Edit tool. Note: the only tools that display a cursor when you move the puck are the sketching tools; you will not, for example, see the Edit tool cursor when it is the active tool and you are driving it from the digitizing board. For tools other than the sketching tools, you must rely on the position of the puck. Mouse events work the same for all tools.

The Output object model

The Objects in the Output area of the object model are used for printing and file export.

Printer and Paper objects

Printer-derived objects are used to invoke the proper driver for printed output according to the user's printer device selection. Internally, Printer objects are created by the print dialog and exist only until the print function has ended (however, the Paper object has printer information, also).

Printer object types correspond to the print engine options offered by the print dialog.

- EmfPrinter—"Windows Printer Driver" in the print dialog. Outputs through the standard Windows printing system.

- ArcPress—Generates output in raster image data format.

- PsDriver—Supports PostScript-compatible output devices. The SpotPlate object is used whenever PostScript color spot plates are called for.

The Paper object (available as a property of Application) holds current printer and sheet attributes. It is used in page layout calculations. Its properties include the following:

- PrinterName represents the current printer name.

- FormName is the name of the current sheet type.

- FormID identifies the current form in terms of a Win32 API DMPAPER_xxx macro value (e.g., 1 = DMPAPER_LETTER).

- Forms returns an enumerator object list of all form types declared by the current printer driver.

- Orientation is the Win32 API DMORIENT_xxx value (DMORIENT_PORTRAIT = 1, DMORIENT_LANDSCAPE = 2).

- PrintableBounds represents the printing area limits of the current output device, given as a rectangle expressed in inches.

Exporter objects

Exporter objects create graphical data files in a variety of standard formats from the current ArcMap document. Their names indicate the format, but note that DibExporter would be used for BMP files ("DIB" = "Device Independent Bitmap").

The procedure for using them is similar for all types:

- Set the output file name (can be the full path designation) into ExportFileName.

- Set the output image size (in pixels) into PixelBounds.

- Call StartExporting, which returns a device context identifier.

- Use MxDocument.ActiveView.Output to draw the desired view region to the export file, using the device context from the previous step.

- Call FinishExporting to complete the file output process.

Working with ArcCatalog

This chapter provides information on how to interact and enhance the elements of the ESRI Object library that relate to ArcCatalog. ArcCatalog provides users a way to assemble all the data they work with in one place. A catalog contains connections to folders on local disks and to shared folders and databases that are available on the network. Typically, users use ArcCatalog to do the following:

• Browse through the contents of their catalog, looking for the map they want to use.

• Preview the contents of a coverage or any other dataset to see if it contains the information they need.

• Organize their maps and data; for example, they might copy a set of maps into a shared folder on the network where everyone in their organization can access them.

The ArcCatalog object model

ArcCatalog lets you assemble all the data you work with in one place. The data is organized in a tree view on one side and a set of views (also known as GxViews) to explore the data. The tree view and the GxViews are tied together within the ArcCatalog application. The ArcCatalog application framework allows developers to extend every aspect of the software such that you can enable your own data types to show them in the tree view alongside ESRI-supported data types. You can also define the behavior for your custom objects. For example, you can create your own custom previews for your data objects and host the custom display into ArcCatalog GxViews (as a new preview type or as a new custom tab).

In general, the ArcCatalog architecture consists of three tiers, each of which is extensible through COM.

The bottommost tier contains the GxObjects themselves. All of these objects support the IGxObject interface as well as other more specific interfaces. The core set of objects are the catalog, disk connection, folder, file, database, and dataset. But this set can be extended easily by providing additional GxObject factories. Basically, whenever a folder is asked for its children, it iterates over all registered GxObject factories and asks them to return GxObjects for the files in the current folder. Custom GxObjects and GxObjectFactories can be written in C++ or VB.

The middle tier contains all the GxViews. These views support IGxView and operate on and off of the GxSelection object (which is owned by the GxCatalog). Each view registers itself as an event sink for the selection object— whenever the selection changes (programmatically or via user action), each view is notified of the change and can update itself accordingly. The core set of views are the tree view, contents view, preview, geographic view, and table view. Preview is unlike any other view in that all it does is host other views within it. Developers can, of course, extend the set of GxViews with their own, written in C++ or VB.

The topmost tier is the application itself. It is basically just a shell that hosts GxViews, although it does have some hardcoded behavior: it always creates a tree view and uses the rest of the main window as a tab control, where each tab represents a different GxView. GxViews can be registered in one of two ways—as a tab view or as a preview. If registered as a tab view, they appear as a separate tab in the main window. If registered as a preview, they are only available with the preview tab. Just like the other tiers, the application itself is extensible using VBA. Scripts and buttons can be added to the basic interface to do just about any task the user wishes.

In addition to the above components, ArcCatalog supports a 'mini' catalog browser that you can enable to browse for data and to save data (this is the same browser that you see in ArcMap's Add Data dialog). The catalog browser supports several object filters to show only the data that you wish to browse. You can also extend the standard GxFilters to support your custom objects. You do this by implementing your own version of the IGxObjectFilter interface.

Adding a new tab to the Views panel

The ArcCatalog Views panel at the right of the application contains three tabs, each of which provides a unique way to see the contents of the selected item in the Catalog tree. The Contents tab lets users see a list of the selected item's contents, the Preview tab lets them see the data contained by the selected item, and the Metadata tab provides a way to see additional information associated with the data.

You may have specifications that require you to implement an additional tab in the Views panel. Your requirements might demand a way to view the selected item in a new way, or they may demand that ArcCatalog handle a file type that's not supported by the existing views.

Let's assume that the specification you've been given is to add a new tab that will allow you to preview text files, ArcInfo AML files, and Rich Text Format (RTF) files. The new tab with the caption, "Text" will appear in the combo box of the Preview tab. When you select one of these file types, clicking the Preview tab will display a panel that previews the file's text.

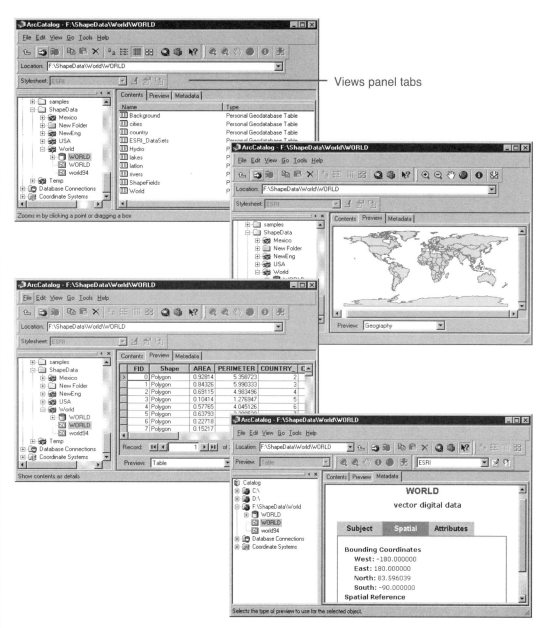

Views panel tabs

In order to create the new view, its tab, and associated behavior, you should supply code to do the following:

1. Create a class that will allow you to display the view and its tab. In this class, you'll implement the methods of the IGxView interface.

2. Handle the Catalog selection event; that is, deal with what happens when the user selects an item in the Catalog tree. In order to handle the selection in the Catalog, you'll declare a variable that can respond to the events of a GxSelection.

3. Design a form that will contain what appears in the view. In this case, your form will contain an RTF control, the Microsoft Rich TextBox Control 6.0 (RICHTX32.OCX), that will display the contents of the file.

```
Option Explicit
Implements IGxView                              (1)
Dim WithEvents g_selectionHandler As GxSelection  (2)
Dim m_catalog As IGxCatalog


Private Sub g_selectionHandler_OnSelectionChanged(ByVal sel As
esriCore.IGxSelection, initiator As Variant)
   PrivateRefresh sel
End Sub


Private Sub IGxView_Activate(ByVal Application As
esriCore.IGxApplication, ByVal Catalog As esriCore.IGxCatalog)
   Set m_catalog = Catalog
   Set g_selectionHandler = Catalog.Selection

   Load frmTextView                             (3)
   PrivateRefresh Catalog.Selection
End Sub


Private Function IGxView_Applies(ByVal Selection As esriCore.IGxObject)
As Boolean
   'Indicate whether or not the currently selected object can be viewed.
   IGxView_Applies = False

   Dim ext As String
   ext = GetExtension(Selection.Name)

   If TypeOf Selection Is IGxFile And (ext = ".txt" Or ext = ".rtf" _
   Or ext = ".aml") Then
      IGxView_Applies = True
   End If
End Function
```

Tip

OnSelectionChanged
This event is available as part of the GxSelection coclass when you declare g_selectionHandler using the WithEvents keyword.

Tip

hWnd
This property supplies the hWnd of the RTF control that displays the contents of the files.

```
Private Property Get IGxView_ClassID() As esriCore.IUID
  Dim uid As New uid
  uid.Value = "TextView.clsTextView"
  Set IGxView_ClassID = uid
End Property

Private Sub IGxView_Deactivate()
  Unload frmTextView
End Sub

Private Property Get IGxView_DefaultToolbarCLSID() As esriCore.IUID
  Set IGxView_DefaultToolbarCLSID = Nothing
End Property

Private Property Get IGxView_hWnd() As esriCore.OLE_HANDLE
  IGxView_hWnd = frmTextView.txtContents.hWnd
End Property

Private Property Get IGxView_Name() As String
  'This label will show up in ArcCatalog's "Preview" combo-box.
  IGxView_Name = "Text"
End Property

Private Sub IGxView_Refresh()
  PrivateRefresh m_catalog.Selection
End Sub

Private Property Get IGxView_SupportsTools() As Boolean
  IGxView_SupportsTools = False
End Property
```

Tip

When you're done

Register the ActiveX DLL and then run Categories.exe in the installation's bin folder. Add the DLL to the ESRI GX Previews component category. Start ArcCatalog. In the Tools menu, select Options and then click the File Types tab. Click Import from Registry and locate the TXT file type; repeat this step to import the RTF file type and then add an AML file type in the File Type dialog's File extension text box. Once you've added these new file types, select a file that is one of these types in the Catalog tree. Click the Preview tab and the panel will display a preview of the text.

```
Private Sub PrivateRefresh(ByVal sel As IGxSelection)
  'If the extension is correct, tell the RTF control to fill itself with
  'the contents of the file.

  Dim ext As String
  ext = GetExtension(sel.Location.Name)

  If ext = ".txt" Or ext = ".rtf" Or ext = ".aml" Then
    frmTextView.txtContents.fileName = sel.Location.FullName
  Else
    frmTextView.txtContents.fileName = ""
  End If
End Sub


Private Function GetExtension(fileName As String) As String
  Dim extPos As Long
  extPos = InStrRev(fileName, ".")
  If extPos > 0 Then
    GetExtension = LCase(Mid(fileName, extPos))
  Else
    GetExtension = ""
  End If
End Function


Private Sub IGxView_SystemSettingChanged(ByVal Flag As Long, ByVal
section As String)

End Sub
```

Using the GxDialog 'mini' catalog browser

In certain situations, you may want to constrain what types of data users can add, open, or save as part of an application. The 'mini' catalog browser provided by GxDialog is available to all application clients, with several ESRI-provided filters (all called GxFilterXxx) that you can use to pick the more common types of objects. In additon you can create your own filter and pass them to the GxDialog by implementing the IGxObjectFilter interface.

In the example provided, the supplied filter restricts selection to point feature classes and then performs an action on each selected object.

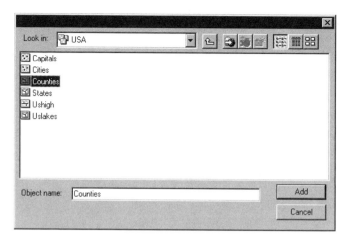

The GxDialog invoked by DoModalOpen without a filter. Note that the ButtonCaption is 'Add' and the Title is blank by default. In addition, AllowMultiSelect is False by default.

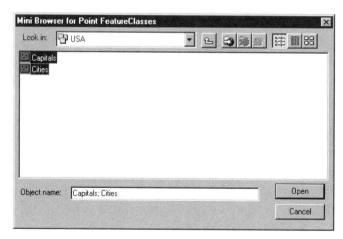

The GxDialog invoked by DoModalOpen with a filter and parameters set as in the example on the following page.

This example, in VBA, displays the GxDialog seen at the bottom of the preceding page. In order to display the 'mini' catalog browser your code should do the following:

1. Declare and establish a GxDialog object.

2. Declare a variable to receive the objects selected in the dialog.

3. Co-create one of the built-in filters if your applicaton requires it.

4. Specify any parameters for the GxDialog.

5. Invoke DoModalOpen or DoModalSave depending on your application requirements.

6. Iterate through the selection, performing the action you want on each selection.

```vba
Sub ShowMiniBrowser()
  Dim bObjectSelected As Boolean
  Dim pGxDialog As IGxDialog
  Set pGxDialog = New GxDialog          ❶
  Dim pEnumGxObject As IEnumGxObject    ❷

  Dim pFilter As IGxObjectFilter
  ' constrain what browser displays
  Set pFilter = New GxFilterPointFeatureClasses   ❸

  With pGxDialog                        ❹
    .AllowMultiSelect = True
    .ButtonCaption = "Open"
    .Title ="Mini Browser for Point FeatureClasses"
    Set .ObjectFilter = pFilter
    bObjectSelected = .DoModalOpen _    ❺
    (ThisDocument.Parent.hWnd, pEnumGxObject)
  End With

  If bObjectSelected = True Then
    Dim pGxObject As IGxObject
    pEnumGxObject.Reset
    Set pGxObject = pEnumGxObject.Next
    Do While (Not pGxObject Is Nothing)   ❻
      MyProc pGxObject.FullName 'MyProc not implemented here
      Set pGxObject = pEnumGxObject.Next
    Loop
  End If
End Sub
```

Working with the Geodatabase   8

This chapter provides information on how to interact and enhance the elements of the ESRI Object Library that relate to the Geodatabase. Typically, in addition to creating new Geodatabases from scratch, users interact with the Geodatabase to do the following:

- Migrate existing data into the Geodatabase.

- Work with subtypes and attribute domains.

- Define relationship classes.

- Manage annotation.

- Work with geometric networks.

- Further refine the Geodatabase by establishing how objects in the database relate to each other.

- Load data into a database schema.

To illustrate how to work with the Geodatabase elements of the ESRI Object Library, this chapter reviews the geodata portion of the object model, Geometry objects, and the Spatial Reference portion of the object model. In addition, several code examples serve to illustrate the elements in use.

The Geodatabase object model

The Geodatabase object model is a generic model for geographic information that can be used with a wide variety of data sources and applications.

The major components of a Geodatabase are Workspaces and Datasets. Understanding this model is key to working with the different kinds of Datasets such as Feature Datasets, Feature Classes, Tables, Grids, Images, and TINs. Here we focus on working with Feature Datasets, Feature Classes, and Tables.

Workspaces, Factories, and Name objects

The principle objects in the model are Workspace factories and Name objects. Workspace factories give out workspaces—you don't CoCreate a workspace. A Workspace is a collection of datasets and provides methods to list, add, delete, copy, and rename the datasets it contains. A Workspace may be implemented as a directory in the file system or as an RDBMS. You need to open a workspace before accessing datasets in that workspace. There are numerous methods to access a workspace from a workspace factory: Create, Open, OpenFromFile.

Workspaces come in various forms:

- ArcInfo Workspace: A directory containing coverages and an Info subdirectory

- Shapefile Workspace: A directory containing ESRI shapefiles

- Access Workspace: A Microsoft Access Database containing Tables and Feature Datasets

- SDE® Workspace: An ArcSDE™ instance containing Tables and Feature Datasets

- Raster Workspace: A workspace containing Grids and Images

- TIN Workspace: A workspace containing TINs

A Name object is an object that specifies an instance of a Geodatabase object. It is a lightweight version of the Geodatabase object it refers to, while still providing access to some of the properties/methods available in the Geodatabase object. From a name object, an instance of the Geodatabase object specified by the name object can be created/returned and vice versa.

A key benefit of name objects being lightweight is performance. For example, feature dataset objects contain a number of instances of feature class objects, whereas feature dataset name objects do not. Name objects also support persistence, either via a stream or by converting the name object into a string. Another use for name objects is that since they can be created independent of their Geodatabase object, they may specify a Geodatabase object that does not yet exist. For example, some geoprocessing operations may generate a new dataset as output, which can be specified by a dataset name object. There are several types of name objects: Workspace, FeatureClass, FeatureDataset, Raster, RelationshipClass, and GeometricNetwork.

Domains are used to constrain the values allowed in any particular attribute for a table, feature class, or subtype. Domains can be shared across feature classes and tables in a Geodatabase. There are two types of domains: RangeDomains, which specify a valid range of values for a numeric attribute, and CodedValueDomains, which specify a valid set of values for any type of attribute.

Datasets

A Dataset is an abstract class that represents both geographic and nongeographic data collections such as tables, feature datasets, grids, and images.

A GeoDataset is an abstract class representing Datasets that have a geographic component; it has a spatial extent and a defined Spatial Reference. FeatureDataset is a subclass of a GeoDataset.

Other subclasses of GeoDatasets include Grids, TINs, and Images.

A FeatureDataset is a Dataset consisting of a set of one or more FeatureClasses. The Feature classes in a FeatureDataset may be independent of each other or may be organized into Networks and Coverages.

A PropertySet is a collection of name–value pairs. A property set can be used to store connection information for an SDE workspace. But a property set can store more than strings—it can store numbers, dates, and even interface pointers.

Tables and rows

There are several classes that are used to access Tables. From a table a cursor can be created, which can examine rows (one at a time). A cursor can look at all the rows or a subset that is defined by a QueryFilter. A QueryFilter holds an SQL "where clause" and fields to extract (SubFields attribute of the QueryFilter). Getting the Fields object will allow you to look at each individual field definition.

FeatureClass and features

Accessing features in a FeatureClass is essentially the same as accessing rows out of a table. You can create a feature cursor allowing you to get access to each feature. A feature cursor can look at all the records or a subset that is defined by a QueryFilter or a SpatialFilter (which is a QueryFilter). A SpatialFilter holds all the properties of a QueryFilter and spatial constraints (e.g., a polygon area that features must spatially reside in).

A RelationshipClass is an association between two object classes; one is the origin class and the other the destination class. The Cardinality of a Relationship class is expressed as an ordered pair of the form (Origin Cardinality– Destination Cardinality).

Examples are 1-1, 1-M, M-1, M-N (OneToOne, OneToMany, ManyToOne, and ManyToMany). A RelationshipClass may be Simple or Composite. A Composite relationship is a 1-to-M relationship between an Origin Class and a Destination Class where the origin class controls the lifetime of the destination class. A Simple relationship is a peer-to-peer relationship where related objects can exist independent of each other.

Validation rules

A Geodatabase supports three broad types of validation rules: attribute validation rules, network connectivity rules, and relationship rules. It is important to understand that these validation rules can be broken; in certain cases, a Geodatabase will permit invalid objects to be stored in the database.

For example, if you have an attribute rule stating that the valid pressure range for a water distribution main in your water network is between 50 and 75 psi, the Geodatabase will not prevent you from storing a value outside of that range. However, a distribution main that has a water pressure outside of this range will be an invalid object in the Geodatabase. The Editor has tools that help you identify invalid features so you can correct them.

The exceptions are edge–edge connectivity rules and coded value attribute rules. In these cases, the Editor takes a more active role when editing features with these rules associated with them.

Searching data

Using QueryFilter

There are two ways data can be searched: via its attributes and spatially. If you search for data spatially, then you will need a shape field in the data source. Both the Table and FeatureClass classes have a search method that returns a cursor to the data requested. To select data via its attributes, set the WhereClause with a valid SQL where clause. To increase performance, you can optionally select which fields to bring across. If you don't select any fields, then all fields are made available.

The recycling argument is used for performance. It allows you to specify whether the same memory address is used to extract each feature. Setting the value to TRUE will increase performance because the same memory will be used when you call NextFeature on the FeatureCursor. In some cases you would like different memory space to be allocated for each Feature in the FeatureCursor; set the value to FALSE in these cases.

SQL WhereClause

The SQL where clause is specific to the underlying database. In general, SQL 92 standard is supported in both Access and SDE databases, but there are cases where slight differences exist among Shapefiles, SDE, and Access. Here are some of them that you may need to be aware of:

- In all databases, the Where Clause is case insensitive with regard to the actual field name and keywords.

  "STATE_NAME LIKE ..." is the same as "state_name like ..."

- Both SDE and Shapefiles are case sensitive with regard to the actual field value that you are searching. But Access is case insensitive.

  For example, WhereClause "State_name = 'Florida'" returns 1 in all cases. "State_name = 'florida'" returns 1 in Access but 0 with Shapefiles and SDE.

- The Like predicate is slightly different in Access vs. Shapefile/SDE.

  In Access, an asterisk symbol (*) is used to match any number of characters, and a question mark (?) is used to match any

single character. With SDE and Shapefiles, the percent (%) symbol is used. For example, "State_Name like 'M*'" will return all states that begin with M in Access. But with SDE and Shapefiles, a WhereClause needs to be modified as "State_Name like 'M%'".

Using SpatialFilters

A spatial search can be performed using a SpatialFilter object on a FeatureClass. The SpatialFilter inherits from the QueryFilter. Therefore, adding a spatial constraint to an existing query will involve defining a SpatialFilter (rather than a QueryFilter), setting the same WhereClause and SubFields methods (if required), and then setting the Spatial Geometry methods.

If you're going to specify SubFields with a SpatialFilter, you must always include the Shape field; otherwise the spatial search will fail.

Retrieving data and accessing field values

Retrieving data is an extension to the searching methods; you must get a table (or feature class) instance and then create a cursor. With the cursor you can execute the method NextRow (or NextFeature). This method can be executed for each record in the cursor. It will return a Row (or a Feature) that you can manipulate. You can test for the end of the cursor by the keyword 'Nothing'. Executing the value method on a successful extraction will enable you to read fields for the current row or feature.

Updating data

There are two ways to update data:

- On an individual-feature or individual-row basis. This is referred to as direct object update.

- For the record in the current cursor position. This is referred to as using an updateable cursor.

The method you choose depends on what level of access you are manipulating features and the speed of access you require.

If you are working with individual features, then you should use direct object updates. This method offers the greatest flexibility and is the simplest one to use. Business rules can be automatically enforced in the Delete and Store methods.

Programmatically editing Geodatabases

If you are going to programmatically edit data, that is, you choose not to use the ArcMap Editor, there are a few rules you must follow in order to ensure that custom object behavior (e.g., network topology maintenance, triggering of geoobject developer defined methods) is correctly invoked in response to the changes your application makes to the database. You must also follow these rules in order to ensure that your changes are made within the multiuser editing/long transaction framework.

Rule 1

Make all changes to the Geodatabase within an Edit Session (i.e., bracketed between StartEditing and StopEditing method calls on the workspace object).

Note 1

This behavior is required for any multiuser update of the database. Starting an Edit Session gives the application a state of the database that is guaranteed not to change except for changes made by the editing application. In addition, starting an Edit Session turns on behavior in the Geodatabase such that a query against the database is guaranteed to return a reference to an existing object in memory if the object was previously retrieved and is still in use. This behavior is required for correct application behavior when navigating between a cluster of related objects while making modifications to objects.

Rule 2

Group your changes into Edit Operations (that is, bracket changes between StartEditOperation and StopEditOperation method calls on the workspace object).

Note 2

You may make all your changes within a single edit operation if so required. Edit Operations can be undone and redone. In the case of SDE, creating at least one edit operation is a requirement, and there is no additional overhead to creating an edit operation.

Rule 3

Use non-recycling search cursors to select objects or fetch objects that are to be updated. Recycling cursors should be used only for drawing by read-only applications.

Note 3

Nonrecycling cursors within an edit session create new objects only if the object to be returned does not already exist in memory.

Rule 4

Always fetch all properties of the object, i.e., query filters should always use '*'.

Note 4

If all properties are not fetched, then object-specific code that is triggered may not find the properties that the method requires.

For example, a geoobject developer might write code to update attributes A and B whenever the geometry of a feature changes. If only the geometry was retrieved, then attributes A and B would be found to be missing within the OnChanged method. This would cause the OnChanged method to return an error, which would cause the Store to return an error and the edit operation to fail.

Rule 5

After changing an object, mark the object as changed (and guarantee that it is updated in the database) by calling Store on the object. Delete an object by calling the Delete method on the object. Set versions of these calls also exist and should be used if the operation is being performed on a set of objects to ensure performance.

Note 5

Calling these methods guarantees that all necessary polymorphic object behavior built into the Geodatabase is executed (for example, updating of network topology and updating of specific columns in response to changes in other columns in ESRI-supplied objects). It also guarantees that developer-supplied behavior in response to messages such as OnDelete and OnChanged is correctly triggered.

Rule 6

Never use Update cursors or Insert cursors to update or insert objects into object and feature classes in an already loaded Geodatabase that has active behavior.

Note 6

Update and Insert cursors are bulk cursor APIs for use during initial database loading. If used on an object or feature class with active behavior, they will bypass all object-specific behavior associated with object creation (such as topology creation) and with attribute/geometry updating (such as automatic recalculation of other dependent columns).

Creating a new SDE workspace

The following VBA code creates a new SDE workspace (connection file) and then opens that workspace.

Tip

Using the Create method
The IWorkspaceFactory's Create method has different results depending on the type of workspace factory. If you are working with SDE, a new connection file (.sde) is created. If you are working with an ArcInfo workspace factory, then a folder with an INFO subfolder is created.

```
Sub CreateSDEWorkSpace()
   Dim pSdeWorkspaceFactory As IWorkspaceFactory
   Dim pSdeWorkspace As IWorkspace
   Dim pConnectionProperties As IPropertySet
   Dim pSdeWorkspaceName As IWorkspaceName
   Dim pName As IName
   Set pConnectionProperties = New PropertySet
   With pConnectionProperties
      .SetProperty "SERVER", "Redarrow"
      .SetProperty "USER", "vtest"
      .SetProperty "INSTANCE", "sde4_ora"
      .SetProperty "PASSWORD", "go"
   End With
   Set pSdeWorkspaceFactory = New SdeWorkspaceFactory
   Set pSdeWorkspaceName = pSdeWorkspaceFactory.Create _
   ("D:\Data", "RedArrow", pConnectionProperties, Application.hWnd)
   Set pName = pSdeWorkspaceName
   Set pSdeWorkspace = pName.Open
End Sub
```

Creating a new feature class

Creating a new feature class that is part of a FeatureDataset involves setting the CLSID for the type of FeatureClass, the creation of a GeometryDef for the shapefield, the definition of the fields that will be in the table, and the creation of the table.

The function presented here takes a FeatureDataset and the name of the FeatureClass and returns a FeatureClass.

```
Public Function CreateFeatureClass(pFeatDS As IFeatureDataset,
strFeatClsName As String) As IFeatureClass
  ' Creates a new Feature Class

  Dim pFeatClsCLSID As IUID
  Set pFeatClsCLSID = New UID
  'Set the CLSID for Simple FeatureClass Types
  pFeatClsCLSID.Value = "{52353152-891A-11D0-BEC6-00805F7C4268}"

  Dim pWS As IWorkspace
  Set pWS = pFeatDS.Workspace

  If Not FeatClsExists(pWS, strFeatClsName) Then

    Dim pFields As IFields
    Set pFields = New Fields

    Dim pFieldsEdit As IFieldsEdit
    Set pFieldsEdit = pFields

    Dim pField As IField
    Dim pFieldEdit As IFieldEdit

    ' create GeometryDef for shape field
    Dim pGeoDef As IGeometryDef
    Set pGeoDef = New GeometryDef
    Dim pGeoDefEdit As IGeometryDefEdit
    Set pGeoDefEdit = pGeoDef
    With pGeoDefEdit
      .AvgNumPoints = 50
      .GeometryType = esriGeometryPolyline
```

```
  .GridCount = 1
  .GridSize(0) = 1000
  .HasM = False
  .HasZ = False
End With

' Set up four field definitions and add fields to the pFields object

'Field 1 Definition
Set pField = New Field
Set pFieldEdit = pField
With pFieldEdit
  .Name = "OID"
  .Type = esriFieldTypeOID
End With
pFieldsEdit.AddField pField

'Field 2 Definition
Set pField = New Field
Set pFieldEdit = pField
With pFieldEdit
  .Name = "Picture"
  .Type = esriFieldTypeBlob
End With
pFieldsEdit.AddField pField

'Field 3 Definition
Set pField = New Field
Set pFieldEdit = pField
With pFieldEdit
  .Name = "Type"
```

```
                        .Type = esriFieldTypeInteger
                      End With
                      pFieldsEdit.AddField pField

                      'Field 4 Definition
                      Set pField = New Field
                      Set pFieldEdit = pField
                      With pFieldEdit
                        .Name = "Shape"
                        .Type = esriFieldTypeGeometry
                        .GeometryDef = pGeoDef
                      End With
                      pFieldsEdit.AddField pField

                      'Create the table
                      Dim pFeatCls As IFeatureClass
                      Set pFeatCls = pFeatDS.CreateFeatureClass(strFeatClsName, pFields, _
                      pFeatClsCLSID, Nothing, esriFTSimple, "Shape", "")

                      Set pField = Nothing
                      Set pFields = Nothing

                      Set CreateFeatureClass = pFeatCls
                    Else
                      Set CreateFeatureClass = Nothing
                    End If

                  End Function
```

Geometry objects

Geometry objects is the subsystem of ArcObjects that handles the geometry, or shape, of features stored in feature classes or other graphical elements. The Geometry for Feature Classes is stored in a table column. Graphical entities in ArcMap also have geometry and have the same properties and methods as shapes stored in feature classes.

The fundamental geometry objects that most users will interact with are Point, MultiPoint, Polyline, and Polygon. They are all creatable objects. Beside those top-level entities are geometries that serve as building blocks for polylines and polygons. Those are Segments, Paths, and Rings. Polylines and polygons are composed of a sequence of connected segments that form a Path. A Segment consists of two distinguished points, the startpoint and the endpoint, and an element type that defines the curve from start to end. The kinds of segments are CircularArc, Line, EllipticArc, and BezierCurve.

All geometry objects have Z, M (measure), and ID values associated with their vertices. In order to use Z's, M's, and ID's, you need to make the objects 'ZAware', 'MAware', and 'IDAware' by using the IZAware, IMAware, and IPointIDAware interfaces.

Topological and Relational Operators can be applied to all fundamental geometries. The Topological Operators include Buffering, Clipping, Cutting, and Intersection methods on geometries. The Relational Operators include the Contain, Cross, Touch, and Within methods.

Working with Geometry objects

The Envelope object holds the information about the spatial extent of geometries. It is a rectangle with the minimum and maximum boundaries for the shape. It exposes the IEnvelope interface to work with the extents.

The Point and Multipoint objects both work with points. The Multipoint object is for points that have been grouped together in a point cluster. Points are zero-dimensional geometries that have x- and y-coordinates, with an optional z and/or m value. Point and MultiPoint both support Topological and Relational operators.

The Path object is a collection of connected segments. It exposes the IPath interface that has methods such as to Generalize or Smooth Polylines or Polygons.

The Polyline object is a collection of paths that can be connected or disjointed. It represents geometry of all linear features. A Polyline is one-dimensional geometry and can have optional M and Z values.

The Polygon object is a collection of rings that bound an area. They are very similar to regions. The simplest form is a polygon with one ring. A more complex form includes nested rings having interiors and islands (exterior rings).

The Ring object is for Polygons. It is a collection of segments that form a closed path. Rings are nonintersecting. The Ring object exposes the IRing and IArea interfaces.

The CircularArc object is for arc segments. An arc has a center point, a radius, and an angle that it spans. The CircularArc object has the ICircularArc interface that exposes the properties of the arc and the IConstructArc to construct new arcs.

The Line object is for line segments. The segment is a straight line connected from the startpoint to the endpoint. The Line object has the ILine and IConstructLine interfaces to get properties and construct new lines.

The EllipticArc object is for elliptical segments. The segment is an ellipse with a startpoint and an endpoint. The object has the IEllipticArc and IConstructEllipticArc interfaces to get properties and construct new ellipses.

The BezierCurve object is for segments with Bezier curves. It has the IBezierCurve and IConstructBezierCurve interfaces to get properties to create the complex curve.

Working with Geometry collections

A GeometryBag is a very lightweight collection object that can store anything that exposes the IGeometry interface. It exposes the IEnumGeometry and IGeometryCollection interfaces. Instances of it are created by methods of the IConstructGeometryCollection interface. Clients can also create them directly.

A GeometryCollection is an interface to handle a collection for a set of geometries. New geometries can be added to an existing collection and/or removed. GeometryCollection can be used to store a set of Geometry pointers to be addressed later in the application.

IPointCollection is an interface to handle a collection of points. It can be applied to Polylines and Polygons.

Setting M values

This VBA code example sets M (measure) values for the selected polylines in an edit session using the ISegmentation interface and the SetMAsDistance method. The M values represent the cumulative lengths.

```
Sub SetMAsDistance()
   On Error GoTo ErrorHandler:
   Dim pApp As IApplication
   Set pApp = Application
   Dim pEditor As IEditor
   Dim pID As New UID
   pID = "esriCore.Editor"
   Set pEditor = pApp.FindExtensionByCLSID(pID)

   Dim pWorkspace As IWorkspace
   Set pWorkspace = pEditor.EditWorkspace

   ' Make sure the data is in Access or ArcSDE ...
   If pWorkspace.Type = esriFileSystemWorkspace Then
      MsgBox "This code does not work for Shapefiles or coverages"
      Exit Sub
   End If

   ' Make sure an Edit session has been started
   If pEditor.EditState <> esriStateEditing Then
      MsgBox "You need to start the edit session", vbInformation, _
      "SetMAsDistance"
      Exit Sub
   End If

   Dim pEdLyrs As IEditLayers
   Dim pLyr As IFeatureLayer

   ' Make sure the target edit layer is PolyLine ...
   Set pEdLyrs = pEditor
   Set pLyr = pEdLyrs.CurrentLayer
```

```
If pLyr.FeatureClass.ShapeType <> esriGeometryPolyline Then
  MsgBox "Current edit layer is not a PolyLine layer.", vbInformation, _
  "SetMAsDistance"
  Exit Sub
End If

Dim pGDef As IGeometryDef
Dim pSRef As ISpatialReference
Dim i As Long

' The Geometry Definition and the Spatial Reference both must be able to
' store M values.

For i = 0 To pLyr.FeatureClass.Fields.FieldCount - 1
  If pLyr.FeatureClass.Fields.Field(i).Type = esriFieldTypeGeometry Then
    Set pGDef = pLyr.FeatureClass.Fields.Field(i).GeometryDef
  End If
Next i

Set pSRef = pGDef.SpatialReference
If Not pSRef.HasMPrecision Or Not pGDef.HasM Then
  MsgBox "This layer cannot store Ms", vbInformation, "SetMAsDistance"
  Exit Sub
End If

' Step through the selected features and set the Ms ...
Dim pEnumFeature As IEnumFeature
Dim pFeat As IFeature
Dim pGeom As IGeometry
Dim pMA As IMAware
Dim pMSeg As IMSegmentation
```

```
    Set pEnumFeature = pEditor.EditSelection
    Set pFeat = pEnumFeature.Next
    If pFeat Is Nothing Then
        MsgBox "There are no selected features.", vbInformation, "Add Ms"
        Exit Sub
    End If

    ' Start an EditOperation (so you can undo the changes)
    pEditor.StartOperation

    While Not pFeat Is Nothing
        Set pGeom = pFeat.ShapeCopy
        Set pMA = pGeom
        pMA.MAware = True 'In order to persist Ms, the geometry must be MAware
        Set pMSeg = pGeom
        pMSeg.SetMsAsDistance False
        Set pFeat.Shape = pGeom
        pFeat.Store
        Set pFeat = pEnumFeature.Next
    Wend

    ' check for the undo SetMAsDistance to roll back the changes.
    pEditor.StopOperation ("SetMAsDistance")
    Exit Sub

ErrorHandler:
    MsgBox Err.Description, vbExclamation, , "SetMAsDistance Error"
    pEditor.StopOperation ("SetMAsDistance")
End Sub
```

Constructing and drawing a circular arc

A circular arc is a kind of Segment. This simple example illustrates how to create points, construct a three point arc through them, and then draw a CircularArc object to the Display that will be erased during the next redraw. To maintain the persistence of the graphic, the code should run in response to the Map's AfterDraw event.

```
Sub DrawCircularArc()
    'Create three points to draw an arc through.
    Dim pPoint1 As IPoint, pPoint2 As IPoint, pPoint3 As IPoint
    Set pPoint1 = New Point
    Set pPoint2 = New Point
    Set pPoint3 = New Point
    pPoint1.PutCoords 200, 200
    pPoint2.PutCoords 200, 300
    pPoint3.PutCoords 300, 300
    'Construct a Three Point Arc.
    Dim pCArc As IConstructCircularArc
    Set pCArc = New CircularArc
    pCArc.ConstructThreePoints pPoint1, pPoint2, pPoint3, False
    Dim pCircArc As ICircularArc
    Set pCircArc = pCArc

    Dim pPolyline As ISegmentCollection
    Set pPolyline = New Polyline
    pPolyline.AddSegment pCircArc

    Dim pRGBcolor As IRgbColor
    Set pRGBcolor = New RgbColor
    pRGBcolor.RGB = vbRed

    Dim pSLSymbol As ISimpleLineSymbol
    Set pSLSymbol = New SimpleLineSymbol
    pSLSymbol.Color = pRGBcolor

    Dim pMxDoc As IMxDocument
    Set pMxDoc = ThisDocument
    Dim pActiveView As IActiveView
```

```
    Set pActiveView = pMxDoc.FocusMap

    With pActiveView.ScreenDisplay
        .StartDrawing 0, esriNoScreenCache
        .SetSymbol pSLSymbol
        .DrawPolyline pPolyline
        .FinishDrawing
    End With
End Sub
```

The Spatial Reference object model

The ArcObjects Spatial Reference subsystem is a set of component classes that provide interfaces to various spatial reference functionalities. You can use these components to create, define, and query spatial reference information of datasets. You can also access them independently of the ArcCatalog and ArcMap applications. This design allows you to implement spatial reference operations in customization environments that are supported by ArcInfo 8 (such as Microsoft Visual Basic and C++).

SpatialReference

One of the primary components of the Spatial Reference object model is the SpatialReference Abstract Class. This Abstract Class supports the ISpatialReference interface, which provides you access to fundamental spatial reference properties of a dataset such as the domain extents, coordinate precision, and coordinate system. For example, you can use ISpatialReference::SetDomain to set the domain extents for a dataset, which establishes the coordinate boundaries for spatial data.

SpatialReferenceInfo

The SpatialReferenceInfo Abstract Class supports the ISpatialReferenceInfo interface, which allows you to obtain the spatial reference information for a dataset. For example, ISpatialReferenceInfo::Name returns the name of a particular coordinate system object. Other properties include Abbreviation, Alias, FactoryCode, and Remarks. Through type inheritance, the ISpatialReferenceInfo properties can be accessed by several other interfaces available within the Spatial Reference object model.

SpatialReferenceEnvironment

The SpatialReferenceEnvironment CoClass is another primary component of the Spatial Reference object model. Managed by the ISpatialReferenceFactory interface, this CoClass helps create the objects that are essential for establishing a dataset's spatial references. The ISpatialReferenceFactory interface supports the largest number of functions among all Spatial Reference object interfaces. Using these tools, you can create custom coordinate systems for datasets using a variety of functions supported by this interface. For example, the creation of a projection object requires the ISpatialReferenceFactory::CreateProjection function followed by an argument specifying the appropriate projection type. ArcObjects provides a list of these supported argument types within your customization environment.

The creation of geographic and projected coordinate system objects requires using different functions supported by the same interface, ISpatialReferenceFactory. For example, to create a geographic coordinate system object, you need to create objects for the name, datum, prime meridian, angular unit, and finally the geographic coordinate system. To create a projected coordinate system object, you would create objects for the name, underlying geographic coordinate system, linear unit, projection, and if necessary, the projection parameters. While each of these methods generates different objects, the process is similar. You can then employ these objects with various interfaces available in other CoClasses.

Another significant function supported by the ISpatialReferenceFactory interface is ISpatialReferenceFactory::CreateESRISpatialReferenceFromPRJ. This method allows the creation of a dataset's spatial reference based on the contents of an existing ArcInfo .prj file. You can implement this functionality for either a geographic or projected coordinate system. Conversely, the

ISpatialReferenceFactory::ExportESRISpatialReferenceToPRJFile method provides a mechanism to output an ArcInfo .prj file from an existing dataset's spatial reference. Both of these methods provide a way to take advantage of existing routines that involve the use of .prj files. They also provide an easy and effective way to exchange spatial reference information through the use of text files.

GeographicCoordinateSystem

The GeographicCoordinateSystem CoClass serves as the underlying spatial reference component for both geographic and projected coordinate system objects. Supported by two interfaces, IGeographicCoordinateSystem and IGeographicCoordinateSystemEdit, this CoClass is essential in establishing a foundation for numerous spatial reference operations. The IGeographicCoordinateSystem interface allows you to obtain spatial reference properties such as a dataset's CoordinateUnit, Datum, PrimeMeridian, or Usage. These properties are useful in determining the characteristics of a geographic coordinate system.

The IGeographicCoordinateSystemEdit interface allows you to establish a geographic coordinate system object based on its objects such as Name, Datum, PrimeMeridian, and coordinateUnit. This is accomplished by using the IGeographicCoordinateSystemEdit::Define method. Other CoClasses possess associations with the IGeographicCoordinateSystem CoClass that are pertinent in the creation of a geographic coordinate system. These CoClasses are Datum, Spheroid, AngularUnit, and PrimeMeridian. Each supports an interface that you can use to obtain properties and an interface that allows you to define the object. For example, you could use an IDatum::Spheroid property to get the name of the dataset's spheroid. Another example is to use the

IPrimeMeridianEdit::Define function to define the longitude origin for a dataset.

ProjectedCoordinateSystem

Similar to the GeographicCoordinateSystem CoClass, the ProjectedCoordinateSystem CoClass provides the functionality to define a projected coordinate system and obtain information about one. Two interfaces are supported by this CoClass, IProjectedCoordinateSystem and IProjectedCoordinateSystemEdit. IProjectedCoordinateSystem allows you to obtain and set properties and execute methods. Some properties include Projection, CoordinateUnit, ScaleFactor, and ParameterCount. The methods supported by this interface include GetParameters, which returns a list of a dataset's projection parameters, and all of the functions available with the ISpatialReference interface through type inheritance.

The IProjectedCoordinateSystemEdit interface provides you a way to establish a projected coordinate system object based on objects such as Name, geographic coordinate system (GCS), projectedUnit, Projection, and if necessary, projection Parameters. This can be accomplished with the IProjectedCoordinateSystemEdit::Define method. Other CoClasses possess associations with the ProjectedCoordinateSystem CoClass that are pertinent to the creation of a projected coordinate system. These CoClasses are LinearUnit, Projection, and Parameter. Each of these CoClasses supports an interface that you can use to obtain properties and an interface that will allow you to define an object. For example, you could use the ILinearUnit::MetersPerUnit property to get the meters per unit value of an existing coordinate unit. Another example is using the IProjection::GetDefaultParameterCount method to return the number of parameters required for a particular projection.

UnknownCoordinateSystem

The UnknownCoordinateSystem CoClass gives you a way to create a spatial reference for a dataset without defining a geographic or projected coordinate system. This is accomplished using the IUnknownCoordinateSystem interface. This functionality is helpful when you possess spatial reference information about a dataset, such as domain extents and false origin and units, but do not need to assign a geographic or projected coordinate system at the time of data creation.

Creating a custom projection

The following code shows how you can use the Spatial Reference objects to create a custom projection (in this case an Albers Equal-Area Conic projection for the USA). The script then creates a new Spatial Reference and uses that to create a new feature dataset in an Access workspace.

```
Sub Albers_Proj()
  ' Projection    ALBERS
  ' Zunits        NO
  ' Units         FEET
  ' Spheroid      CLARKE1866
  ' Xshift        0.0000000000
  ' Yshift        0.0000000000
  ' Parameters
  '         29 30  0.000  /* 1st standard parallel
  '         45 30  0.000  /* 2nd standard parallel
  '         -96  0  0.000   /* central meridian
  '         37 30  0.000  /* latitude of projection's origin
  '         0.00000     /* false easting (meters)
  '         0.00000     /* false northing (meters)

  ' Create a new spatial reference environment object. QI for its
  ' ISpatialReference factory interface. This spatial reference factory
  ' is what is used to create all spatial reference objects.
  Dim pSpatRefFact As ISpatialReferenceFactory
  Set pSpatRefFact = New SpatialReferenceEnvironment

  ' Create a Projection object by declaring an interface, then use
  ' ISpatialReferenceFactory::CreateProjection to create a pre-defined
  ' projection object, in this case Albers.
  Dim pProjection As IProjection
  Set pProjection = _
  pSpatRefFact.CreateProjection(esriSRProjection_Albers)

  ' Create a PrimeMeridian object, specifying "Greenwich" as the
  ' Prime Meridian type in the CreatePrimeMeridian method
  Dim pPrimMer As IPrimeMeridian
```

```
Set pPrimMer =
pSpatRefFact.CreatePrimeMeridian(esriSRPrimeM_Greenwich)

' Create a Unit object by declaring an interface, then specifying
' 'AmericanFoot' as the UnitType in the CreateUnit method
Dim pLinUnit As IUnit
Set pLinUnit = pSpatRefFact.CreateUnit(esriSRUnit_AmericanFoot)

 ' Create a Unit object by declaring an interface, then specifying
' 'Degree' as the UnitType in the CreateUnit method
Dim pAngUnit As IUnit
Set pEnumAngUnit = pSpatRefFact.CreateUnit(esriSRUnit_Degree)

' To create a new geographic coordinate system object,
' declare IGeographicCoordinateSystem, then create a new
' GeographicCoordinateSystem object. QI for
' IGeographicCoordinateSystemEdit; use Define to set its properties.

Dim pGeogCoordSys As IGeographicCoordinateSystem
Set pGeogCoordSys = New GeographicCoordinateSystem
Dim pGeogCoordSysEdit As IGeographicCoordinateSystemEdit
Set pGeogCoordSysEdit = pGeogCoordSys
pGeogCoordSysEdit.Define Name:="GCS_Albers", Datum:=pDatum, _
PrimeMeridian:=pPrimMer, geographicUnit:=pAngUnit

' To create the new projected coordinate system object,
' declare IProjectedCoordinateSystem,
' then create a new ProjectedCoordinateSystem object.
' QI for IProjectedCoordinateSystemEdit,
' and use Define to assign it its properties.
```

```
Dim pProjCoordSys As IProjectedCoordinateSystem
Set pProjCoordSys = New ProjectedCoordinateSystem
Dim pProjCoordSysEdit As IProjectedCoordinateSystemEdit
Set pProjCoordSysEdit = pProjCoordSys

pProjCoordSysEdit.Define Name:="PCS_Albers", gcs:=pGeogCoordSys, _
projectedUnit:=pLinUnit, Projection:=pProjection

' This particular projection has 6 parameters:
With pProjCoordSys
    .StandardParallel1 = 29.5 ' 1st standard parallel
    .StandardParallel2 = 45.5 ' 2nd standard parallel
    .CentralMeridian = -96 ' central meridian
    .LatitudeOfOrigin = 36.5 ' latitude of projection's origin
    .FalseEasting = 0 ' false easting (meters)
    .FalseNorthing = 0' false northing (meters)
End With

' Create a new SpatialReference and associate the new projected
' coordinate system with it.
Dim pNewSpatRef As ISpatialReference
Set pNewSpatRef = pProjCoordSys

' set the false origin and units for the spatial reference
pNewSpatRef.SetFalseOriginAndUnits -1156788, -10562324, 98

' create a new Access database
Dim pPropset As IPropertySet
Set pPropset = New PropertySet
pPropset.SetProperty "Database", "c:\temp\custproj"
```

```
Dim pAcFact As IWorkspaceFactory
Dim pAcworkspaceName As IWorkspaceName
Set pAcFact = New AccessworkspaceFactory
Set pAcworkspaceName = pAcFact.Create("c:\temp", "custproj", _
pPropset, Application.hwnd)

' create a new feature dataset in the Access database using the newly
' created spatial reference (which has the custom coordinate system)
Dim pACWS As IWorkspace
Dim pName As IName
Set pName = pACworkspaceName
Set pACWS = pName.Open

Dim pAcFeatWS As IFeatureWorkspace
Set pAcFeatWS = pACWS

pAcFeatWS.CreateFeatureDataset "USA_Albers", pNewSpatRef

End Sub
```

Working with CASE tools

9

Presented as a tutorial, this chapter contains information about working with industry-standard CASE tools to assist in the process of defining custom features, creating code to add custom behavior, and creating a geodatabase schema.

Getting started

The CASE tools allow you to create custom features that extend the data model of ArcInfo 8. Object-oriented design tools (OOA&D) can be used to create object models that represent the design of your custom features. These tools make use of the Unified Modeling Language (UML) to create designs. Based on these models the CASE tools will help you create COM classes that implement the behavior of the custom features and database schemas in which custom feature properties are maintained.

The CASE tools consist of two major activities: code generation and schema generation. The former is used to create the behavior, while the latter is used to create schemas in geodatabases. In this tutorial you'll create an object model with custom features, create code adding custom behavior, and create a geodatabase schema.

The tutorial focuses on code generation and object model creation to meet such an objective. For a detailed discussion on how to create other geodatabase elements using UML (such as subtypes, domains, connectivity and relationship rules) refer to *Building a Geodatabase*.

What you'll do

In this tutorial you'll create two custom features commonly used in cadastral systems: a parcel and a building. For parcel features you'll store the actual parcel value and the sum of the value of all the buildings in the parcel. For building features you'll store the number of floors, height, and building value.

You'll create a relationship class in the geodatabase to keep track of the buildings contained in a parcel. This will permit the custom features to maintain their relationship automatically, for example, when a new building is created or when an existing building is moved.

You'll also create a simple custom validation rule for buildings: the height must be at least the number of floors times 10 feet.

The UML diagram on the opposite page depicts the object model that will be built during the tutorial.

What you'll need

To follow this tutorial you'll need ArcInfo 8, a UML design tool such as Visio Enterprise, and Developer Studio 6.0. You will need two to three hours of focused time to complete the tutorial.

Start by making a copy of the tutorial folder to a working folder, for example, to C:\Temp\Tutorial (the default installation folder is C:\Program Files\Esri\ArcInfo\casetools\Tutorial).

The tutorial folder contains the following:

- A Personal SDE database with spatial data (SampleDB.mdb).

- An empty Microsoft Repository (Repository.mdb).

- A source folder where code will be generated. It already contains a couple files with helper functions.

- A folder with the solution.

The tutorial assumes you are familiar with ArcInfo 8, in particular with the geodata access objects C++, ATL, and COM.

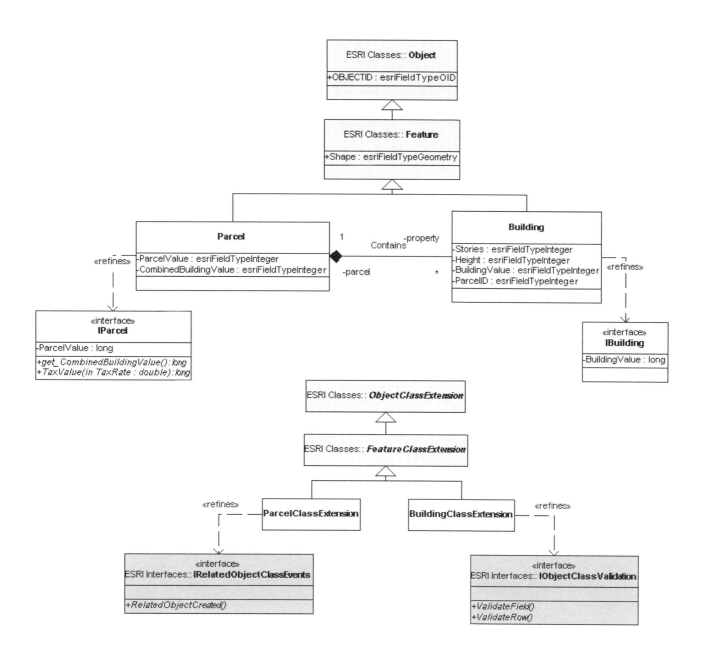

Designing the object model

You represent your object models by creating new UML diagrams in Visio Enterprise. The following sections will guide you through the creation of the object model.

Creating a new model

In Visio you create a new document by choosing a template. The ArcInfo UML Model template diagram contains the information needed to create your object models.

To create the new document

1. Start Visio.

2. Double-click the ArcInfo UML Model (Ent) template file (the default installation path is C:\Program Files\Esri\ArcInfo\Casetools\Uml Models).

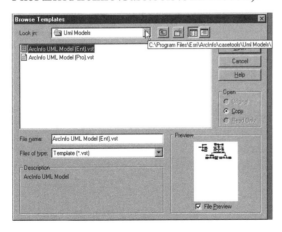

Creating a new ArcInfo UML Model from Visio template

The ArcInfo UML Model

The ArcInfo UML Model contains the relevant parts of the geodata access components needed for the creation of custom features. The object model has four packages: Logical View, ESRI Classes, ESRI Interfaces, and User Features. These UML packages act as directories where different parts of the entire object model are maintained. The Logical View package is the root level and contains the other three packages.

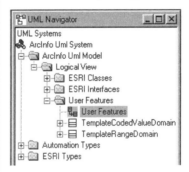

Packages in Visio template

A package contains any number of UML elements such as other packages, classes, interfaces, and diagrams. Notice you are seeing the User Features diagram, which belongs to the User Features package. There is no limit to the number of packages an object model may contain.

To open the ESRI Classes diagram

1. Click the plus sign by the ESRI Classes package.

2. Double-click the ESRI Classes diagram.

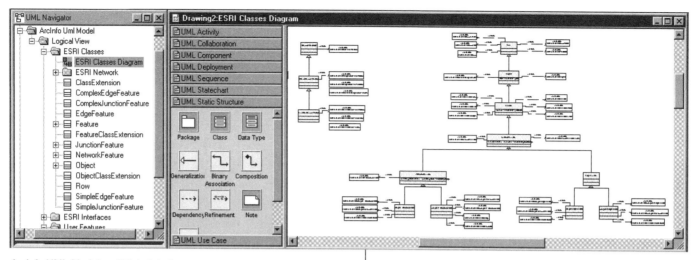

ArcInfo UML Model and Visio Interface

As mentioned before, the UML classes in this diagram represent COM classes that belong to the geodata access components of ArcInfo. These COM classes provide services through interfaces. For example, Feature implements the interface IFeatureDraw. ArcMap asks a feature to draw itself using the method Draw() in the interface IFeatureDraw. A UML refinement is used to express the relationship between the class and the implemented interface (Tip: To show the operations in an interface, right-click the interface and then click suppress operations).

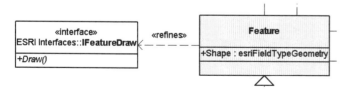

Feature implements IFeatureDraw

Notice classes such as Row, Object, and Feature are defined inside the ESRI Classes package. Interfaces like IFeatureDraw are defined in the ESRI Interfaces package. Diagrams also belong to specific packages; for example, the ESRI Classes Diagram belongs to the ESRI Classes package.

Classes inherit from other classes. For example, Feature inherits from Object, meaning Feature 'is a kind of' Object. A UML generalization is used to express this relationship.

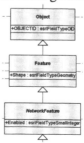

Inheritance chain in ESRI classes

How can a child class be a kind of a parent class? By providing the same services the parent class provides. Since COM classes provide services through interfaces, child classes agree to implement the same interfaces their parent implements. In the sample, Feature implements all the interfaces implemented by Object.

The generalization relationship is 'daisy-chained', so NetworkFeature implements all the interfaces Feature does including those implemented by Object.

User-defined custom features are objects (nonspatial), simple features or network features. Parcel and building will inherit from Feature in the tutorial object model, and thus they will agree to be simple features, implementing all the interfaces that Feature does.

Creating a custom feature

You will create a UML class that represents the parcel custom feature. The information you enter will be used by the schema wizard to create a feature class in a geodatabase. It will also be used to generate C++ stub code where custom behavior can be implemented.

User-defined features should not be defined inside the ESRI Classes or ESRI Interfaces packages. The User Features package should be used instead (or any other package created by the user). To create the parcel custom feature, do the following:

1. In the UML Navigator, double-click on the User Features diagram.

2. From the ESRI Classes package, drag and drop the Object class onto the diagram.

3. From the ESRI Classes package, drag and drop the Feature class onto the diagram.

Notice Visio automatically adds a generalization relationship between Object and Feature, as defined in the ESRI Classes diagram. It is easier to think of the model as maintained inside the UML Navigator and displayed through static structure diagrams.

This is why the same object or relationship can be shown in several different diagrams, even if the object and the diagram don't belong to the same package. Notice the classes just added belong to the ESRI Classes package—hence the name ESRI Classes::Object, but the diagram belongs to the User Features package.

4. From the UML Static Structure stencil, drag and drop a new class onto the diagram.

5. Drag and drop a generalization onto the diagram and connect the new class to Feature.

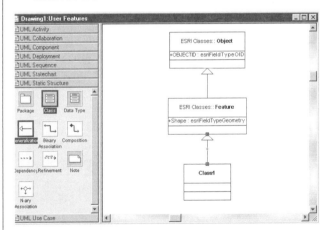

Creating a new feature class

You can set the properties of the newly created class.

1. Double-click the class to open its properties.

2. Type Parcel in the Name box.

3. Click the Attributes tab.

4. Click New to create a new attribute.

5. Type ParcelValue in the Name box.

Attribute Property Page of UML Property Editor

6. Click the Type dropdown and click esriFieldTypeInteger to set the field type.

7. Click OK.

8. Repeat steps 4 through 7 to add a second attribute, CombinedBuildingValue. Set its type to be esriFieldTypeInteger.

9. Click the Tagged Values tab for the class (you'll have to scroll right through the available tabs).

A tagged value is a keyword–value pair that may be attached to any model element. The keyword is called a tag and represents a property applicable to one or many elements. Both the keyword and value are strings, allowing you to attach arbitrary information to models.

1. Click New to create a new tagged value.

2. Type GeometryType in the Tag box.

3. Type esriGeometryPolygon in the Value box.

4. Click OK.

5. Click OK.

You have created a class that represents the parcel custom feature. The schema wizard will create a feature class based on the information you just entered. The feature class will store polygons as specified by the geometry type tagged value, and the UML attributes (ParcelValue and CombinedBuildingValue) will be used to create two fields in the feature class table.

Notice OBJECTID and Shape are inherited UML attributes (from object and feature, respectively). The feature class will have these two fields as well.

Repeat steps 4 through 9 and then steps 1 through 5 of the tagged value steps to create a second class. Name the class Building and add the following attributes:

Name	Type
Stories	esriFieldTypeInteger
Height	esriFieldTypeInteger
BuildingValue	esriFieldTypeInteger
ParcelID	esriFieldTypeInteger

The ParcelID attribute will be used to store foreign keys for a relationship class. You'll work with a relationship class in a subsequent section of the tutorial. This is how your model should look.

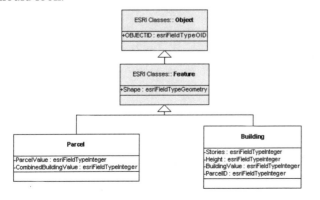

Creating an interface

As mentioned before, Parcel and Building will behave like features because they will implement all the interfaces implemented by Feature. Clients for such interfaces include ArcMap, ArcCatalog, and the geodata access components themselves.

But what if an application requires calculation of the parcel's tax value based on the buildings it contains, its own value, and a given tax rate? Such calculation could be done by an application querying for the values from the database. But what if the same calculation is needed for several applications? In that case it would be more efficient to perform the calculation inside the Parcel custom feature and provide the service through a user-defined interface.

In this step you'll create a user-defined interface for the parcel feature IParcel. The interface will provide a convenient way to retrieve or write the parcel's value, a read-only property to retrieve the value of all the buildings in the parcel, and a method to calculate the parcel's tax value.

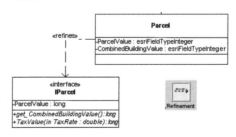

Parcel implements IParcel

To create the interface

1. Drag and drop a new class onto the diagram.

2. Double-click the new class to open its properties.

3. Type IParcel in the Name box.

4. Click the Stereotype dropdown and then click interface.

5. Click the Attributes tab.

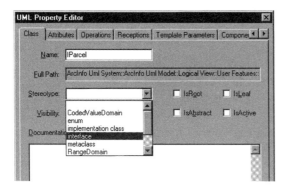

6. Click New to add a new attribute.

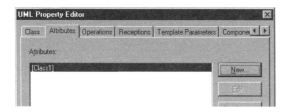

7. Type ParcelValue in the Name box.

8. Click the Type dropdown and then click long to set the attribute type.

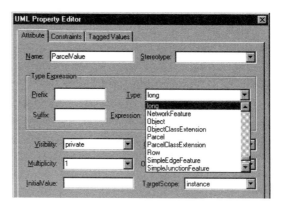

9. Click OK.

An Operation is a service that an instance of a class may be requested to perform. The behavior of a class is represented by a set of operations. Each operation has a name and a list of arguments. In the next few steps, you'll add a new operation.

1. Click the Operation tab.

2. Click New to add a new operation.

3. Type get_CombinedBuildingValue in the Name box (more on the get_ prefix in a subsequent section).

4. Click the Return Type dropdown and then click long to set the operation's returned type.

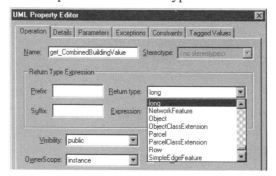

5. Click OK.

6. Click New to add a second operation.

7. Type TaxValue in the Name box. (Note: The name is case sensitive, so type it as shown).

8. Click the Return Type dropdown and click long to set the operation's returned type.

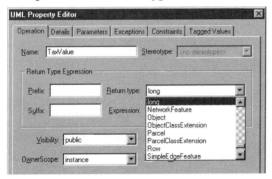

A parameter is an unbound variable that can be changed, passed, or returned. A parameter may include a name, type, and direction of communication. Parameters are used to specify operations, messages, events, templates, and more. In this section of the tutorial, you'll create a new parameter.

1. Click the Parameters tab.

2. Click New to create a new parameter.

3. Type TaxRate in the Name box (case sensitive).

4. Click the Type dropdown and click double to set the parameter type.

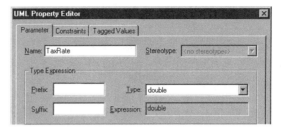

5. Click OK.

6. Click OK.

7. Click OK.

8. Drag and drop a Refinement onto the diagram and connect Parcel to its interface.

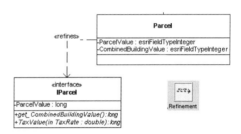

Notice the types used in custom features (esriFieldTypeInteger and the like) are different than the types used in interfaces (long, double, etc.). The types in custom features are used to create fields in feature classes, whereas the types in the interfaces will be used for code generation and therefore are restricted to C++/Automation types (esriFieldTypeInteger is a long integer).

A UML attribute in an interface will be code generated into a mutator/accessor pair (or property put/property get pair). For example, this is the IDL code generated for ParcelValue:

```
[propget] HRESULT ParcelValue([out, retval]
long* ParcelValue);

[propput]  HRESULT ParcelValue([in] long
ParcelValue);
```

The get_CombinedBuildingValue UML operation is a read-only property for the CASE tools. The code generation wizard will recognize the 'get_' prefix of the operation and will generate a COM property of the form (IDL):

```
[propget] HRESULT CombinedBuildingValue([out,
retval] long * value);
```

It becomes a read-only property because there is no propput being generated. Similarly, write-only properties can be created by using the prefix 'put_'.

The TaxValue UML operation is a standard COM method. Its IDL signature looks like this:

```
HRESULT TaxValue([in] double TaxRate, [out,
retval] TaxValue);
```

The building class will also have a user-defined interface. This interface will provide a convenience accessor/mutator pair to the BuildingValue property.

To add the interface

1. Repeat steps 1 through 4 to create the interface, using IBuilding as the name.

2. Repeat steps 5 through 9 to add a new attribute, using BuildingValue as the name and long as the type.

3. Click OK.

4. Drag and drop a Refinement onto the diagram and connect Building to its interface IBuilding.

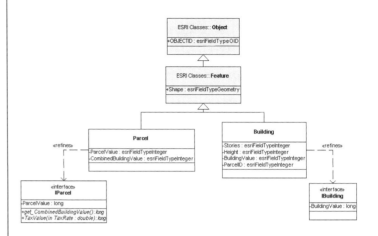

Creating a RelationshipClass

In order to maintain the appropriate relationship between features, you must create the relationship class Contains, which associates parcels to buildings.

To create the relationship class

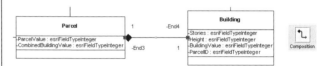

1. Drag and drop a new composite association onto the diagram.

2. Connect the left-hand side of the association to the parcel class and the right-hand side to the building class.

3. Double-click the association to open its properties.

4. Type Contains in the Name box.

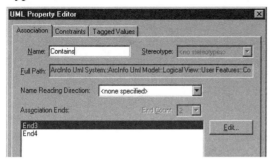

5. Double-click the End3.

6. Type parcel in the Name text box (notice the multiplicity is 1).

7. Click OK.

8. Double-click the End4.

9. Type property in the Name text box. Click the multiplicity dropdown and then click *.

10. Click OK.

11. Click the Tagged Values tab.

12. Click New to add a new tagged value.

13. Type OriginPrimaryKey in the tag box.

14. Type OBJECTID in the value box.

15. Click OK.

16. Repeat steps 12 through 15 to create a second tagged value. Use OriginForeignKey as the tag and ParcelID as the value.

17. Repeat steps 12 through 15 once again to create a third tagged value. Use Notification as the tag and esriRelNotificationBoth as the value.

18. Click OK.

19. Right-click the association and then click Show Name.

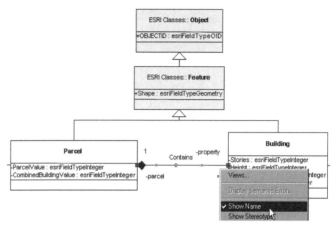

The schema creation wizard will use the information in the UML association to create a relationship class in the geodatabase named Contains. The relationship class type will be composite (in contrast to simple) types, its cardinality will be one to many (1-M), and both objects will be notified when a peer object is changed (notification).

In a composite relationship, one of the objects controls the lifetime of the associated objects. In the tutorial case the parcel controls the lifetime of the buildings, so when a parcel is deleted, the buildings inside will be deleted as well. This behavior is not present in peer-to-peer or simple relationship classes.

Relationship classes are implemented in the underlying geodatabase using primary and foreign key fields in the feature classes' tables. The primary key for the relationship is the parcel's OBJECTID field (inherited from Object in the model), and the foreign key is the building's ParcelID field.

Creating a ClassExtension

A class extension is a COM class that implements behavior that pertains to the whole set of custom features in a feature class, in contrast to behavior that belongs to a singular custom feature. For example, the property inspector of a feature is implemented by the class extension. The same property inspector is used for all instances in the feature class.

CASE tools will find class extensions by naming convention. A valid class extension name is made up of the class name followed by the string 'ClassExtension' (for example, BuildingClassExtension).

Class extensions are created in the same way custom features are created, by defining new UML classes that inherit from classes in the ESRI Classes diagram. The building class extension will contain the code for a custom validation rule. To create it do the following:

1. From the ESRI Classes package, drag and drop ObjectClassExtension onto the diagram.

2. From the ESRI Classes package, drag and drop FeatureClassExtension onto the diagram.

3. From the UML Static Structure stencil, drag and drop a new class onto the diagram.

4. Drag and drop a generalization onto the diagram and connect the new class to FeatureClassExtension.

5. Double-click the class to open its properties.

6. Type BuildingClassExtension in the Name box.

7. Click OK.

8. From the ESRI Interfaces package, drag and drop IObjectClassValidation onto the diagram.

9. Drag and drop a new refinement onto the diagram and connect the new class extension to the interface (notice the direction of the relationship).

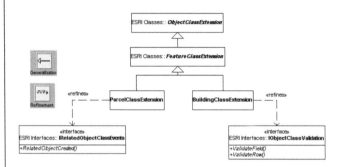

The geodata access components allow for the specification of rules features must comply with. There are different types of rules, for example, a range domain specifies the minimum and maximum values a field can have. Other types of rules include coded value domains, connectivity rules, and relationship rules. All these rules are defined through parameters.

However, there are rules that can't be defined through parameters easily, for example, a rule that includes some sort of spatial constraint (no industry on residential zones) or a rule that involves the value of several feature properties (height >= stories * 10ft). These custom validation rules can be created in the class extension of a feature class, as the implementation of IObjectClassValidation.

When validation is requested, ArcInfo first verifies the rules defined through parameters (domains, connectivity, etc.), then it looks for a class extension. If the class extension is found, and it implements IObjectClassValidation, the methods in the interface are called.

Follow the same procedure to create the parcel class extension. This time grab the IRelatedObjectClassEvents interface from the ESRI Interfaces package. The RelatedObjectCreated method will be used to set the relationship between a new building and its parent parcel. It is the parcel class extension that is going to be 'watching' for new buildings.

You can also create custom interfaces for class extensions whose clients are user applications. Such interfaces are created in the CASE tools in exactly the same way you create an interface for a custom feature.

Each class extension will be another COM class inside the DLL created upon compilation of the C++ project.

Take a couple of minutes now to make sure your model is correct (check attribute names and types for example). Use the model at the beginning of the tutorial as a sample. Save your UML diagram at this time.

UML modeling summary

You are finished with the modeling of the custom features. Notice the following in your diagram.

New ArcInfo UML models are created based on a template.

- Custom features are defined using UML classes.
- User-defined features inherit from classes in the template.

- User-defined features should be created in the User Features package or under other User-defined packages.
- Custom features implement interfaces. The relationship is expressed through a UML refinement.
- Interfaces are UML classes stereotyped as <<interface>>.
- Types in UML classes representing custom features are of the form esriFieldTypeXXX.
- Types in UML classes representing interfaces are restricted to COM/Automation types.
- Attributes in classes are used by the schema wizard to create fields in the feature class.
- Attributes in interfaces are used by the code generation wizard to create propput/propget pairs.
- Relationship classes require primary and foreign keys.
- Tagged values are used to fully specify model elements (for example, GeometryType, OriginPrimaryKey).

Exporting a model to the Repository

The Microsoft Repository supports the storage of a great deal of information related to the development of software including object models created using UML. The CASE tools take advantage of this feature to support any modeling tool that writes to the Repository.

To export the model to a Repository

1. Click the UML menu and then click Export.

2. In the UML Export dialog's Repository text box, type the name of an existing or new Access database or click Browse to navigate to it.

3. Type the name of the model as it will be stored in the repository.

4. Click OK to export the UML model.

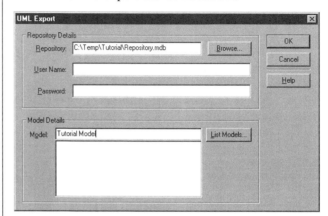

The whole model, including the objects and interfaces in the ESRI packages, is exported to the Repository. Both code and schema will be created using that version of the model.

It might be helpful to have a printed copy of the UML model at hand while following the remaining of the tutorial.

Generating code

You use the code generation wizard to create stub code for the custom features in your object models. The wizard is an Add-In to Developer Studio that will create a C++ project for you. The code generated is based on the Active Template Library (ATL), a framework designed by Microsoft to facilitate COM programming in C++.

Upon compilation of the project, a Dynamic Link Library (DLL) with COM classes will be created. Custom features in the model selected for code generation will become COM classes in the DLL, along with a COM class for the associated class extension, if one exists.

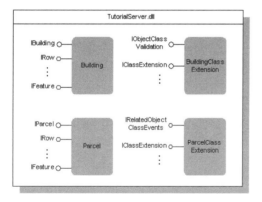

Adding the code generation wizard to Developer Studio

To load the code generation wizard Add-In

1. Start Developer Studio.

2. Click tools and then click Customize.

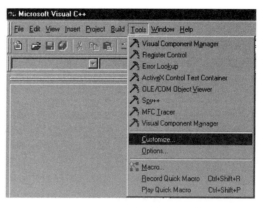

3. Click the Add-ins and Macro Files tab.

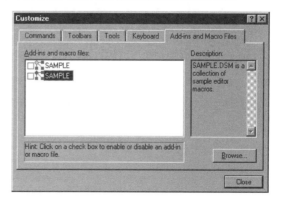

4. Click Browse to search for the add-in (the default installation directory is C:\Program Files\Esri\ArcInfo\bin).

5. Click CodeGenWiz.dll (make sure the file type is DLL).

6. Click Close.

The ESRI code generation Add-In should be loaded now.

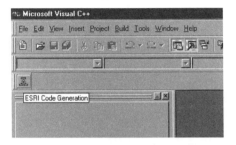

Overview of the Code Generation

The wizard will guide you through the following steps:

- Connect to the Repository.
- Select the Object Model.
- Select the custom features to generate code for.
- Define properties for each custom feature.
- Specify the output C++ project.

Once finished, you will have a C++ project ready to compile where all custom features behave just like a standard geodata access feature. You can then modify each custom feature to include specific behavior.

Connecting to the Repository

Launch the wizard in Developer Studio. Click Next to skip the introduction step and then click Browse to select the

repository database (for example, C:\Temp\Tutorial\Repository.mdb). Click Next to continue.

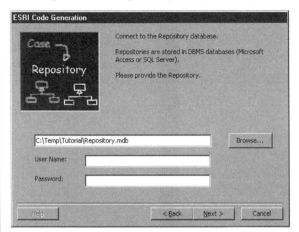

Selecting the object model

A repository database can contain several object models. Select the tutorial model and click Next. At this point the wizard reads the object model from the repository.

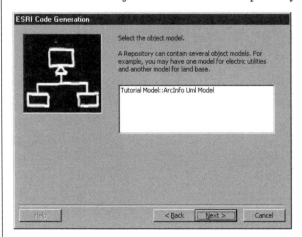

Defining the custom features to create

The wizard will display your object hierarchy in a tree view. Here's where you'll select the custom features you want to create code for. For this example you'll generate code for all the custom features in the model.

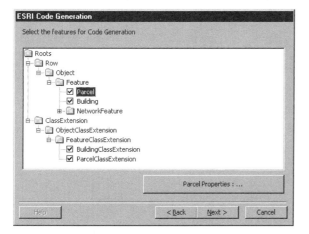

Defining custom feature properties

The behavior of a custom feature is the code behind the properties and methods of the interfaces it supports. The code generation properties of a custom feature allow you to define where the custom behavior will be placed.

1. Double-click Parcel to open its properties.

   The Local Interfaces tab shows the definition of IParcel, the only local interface of parcel in the model. The lower portion provides the IDL definition of the interface members. All the information needed for code generation regarding local interfaces is defined in the model. This tab is designed to let you verify that information.

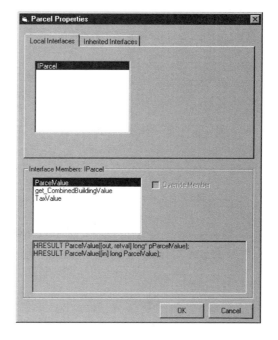

2. Click the Inherited Interfaces tab.

This tab displays the interfaces the Parcel custom feature must implement because it inherits from Feature. By clicking the name of the interface in the upper grid, the appropriate member information is displayed in the bottom part of the form.

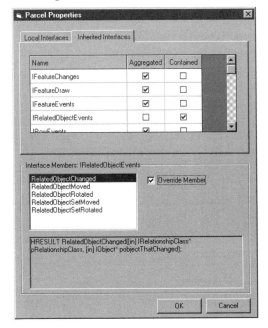

The code generation wizard will include the parent of Parcel (feature), inside the Parcel COM class, in such a way that each time a new instance of Parcel is created, a new instance of the inner feature will be created as well.

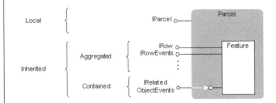

This technique allows the developer to reuse the implementation of all the interfaces Feature implements by either exposing the inner object's implementation directly (aggregation) or by forwarding calls to the inner instance (containment). The client of the COM class has no knowledge about this architecture, and to it, all interfaces look as though they've been implemented by the Parcel COM class.

When an interface is contained, each property or method of the interface can either be forwarded to the inner object or entirely overwritten by the outer object. In the case of the parcel, the only interface we want to contain is IRelatedObjectEvents. In methods such as RelatedObjectChanged we will write custom behavior. All other interfaces will be exposed directly from the inner feature COM class.

To contain the interface and override the methods

1. Click the contained check box for IRelatedObjectEvents.

2. Click the RelatedObjectChanged method.

3. Click Override member check box.

4. Repeat steps 2 and 3 for the RelatedObjectSetMoved method.

5. Click OK.

The same considerations apply for Building. However, this custom feature can reuse Feature's implementation of all the interfaces, so all the inherited interfaces will be aggregated.

Class extensions are a special case in one aspect: they inherit from abstract classes. Notice in your UML model that ClassExtension, ObjectClassExtension, and FeatureClassExtension are abstract classes (the UML convention is to present the class name in italics). In this case, there is no concrete COM class we can embed inside the user-defined class, that is, inside the class extensions for building and parcel.

1. Double-click the Building class extension.

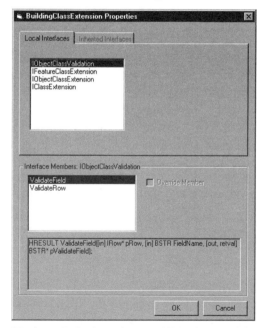

Notice all the interfaces will be implemented locally, so all of them are shown in the Local Interfaces tab. No

interfaces are going to be aggregated or contained, so the Inherited Interfaces tab is disabled.

Notice also the optional interface IObjectClassValidation you added to the UML model is shown as a Local Interface. The method ValidateRow will be used to create the custom validation rule for buildings.

2. Click OK to close the dialog.

3. Double-click ParcelClassExtension to open its properties.

Notice it will implement the optional interface IRelatedObjectClassEvents, just as you specified it in the UML model. The RelatedObjectCreated method will be used to handle the creation of a new building.

4. Click OK to close the dialog.

5. Click Next to continue with the code generation process.

Defining the output Developer Studio project

As the last step of the code generation process, the wizard prompts you to define the output Developer Studio/C++ project. Several files will be created along the project file, so you are better off using a separate folder.

1. Click Define Output Project.

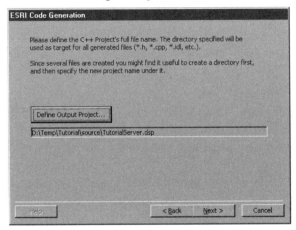

2. Move to the output folder (for example, C:\Temp\Tutorial\source).

3. Type TutorialServer in the File Name box.

4. Click Save.

5. Click Next.

6. Click Finish.

At this point the wizard will generate a Developer Studio project and workspace you can open. The compilation of the project will generate a COM DLL that contains COM classes for the classes in the model: Parcel, Parcel class extension, Building, and Building class extension. The name of the DLL will be TutorialServer, the name of the C++ project.

Adding custom behavior

The following pages will help you add C++ code to implement the behavior for parcels, buildings, and their class extensions. Comments and lengthy lines may appear differently in the book than in the files on disk due to restrictions imposed by the book format.

Generated code

Let's start by browsing through the code just generated. In Developer Studio click the FileView tab and expand the tree so all files are visible. Here is a small description of them (for further details on the project outline, refer to the ATL documentation or any of the books available on ATL).

A number of support files are created such as TutorialServer.cpp, TutorialServer.rc, and TutorialServer.def. These files provide services such as registration and unregistration of the COM classes in your DLL.

The file StdAfx.h contains a #import statement that incorporates information from the esriCore type library. The content of the type library is converted into C++ classes that ease the use of ESRI COM classes and interfaces when writing the behavior.

It is through these wrapper classes that we use the COM classes of the geodata access components. For example, we can write the following code to create an instance of a field object:

```
// IFieldPtr wrapper class
IFieldPtr ipField(CLSID_Field);
```

Another interesting file in your project is TutorialServer.idl. This file has metadata of the contents of your project. Notice the interfaces are defined, and then, inside a type library, all the COM classes are defined too, along with the interfaces they implement. Notice also the custom features implement all the interfaces' feature implements, although you can't tell the difference between aggregated and contained interfaces. This is how a client will see your custom features.

For each COM class a registration file is created, for example, Parcel.rgs. This script creates the registry keys and values so the COM class is correctly registered in the system's registry. It includes registering the parcel COM class in a component category: the custom features component category. Class extensions COM classes (for example, the parcel class extension) are registered in the class extensions component category in the same way.

You also get the header and source files for the classes in the UML model, for example, the header file Parcel.h and the source file Parcel.cpp. In the header file you can recognize a number of ATL macros being used, among them the ones defining the COM_MAP. It is apparent the parcel COM class implements IParcel and IRelatedObjectEvents locally and aggregates any other interface implemented by the inner object (feature).

```
BEGIN_COM_MAP(Parcel)
    COM_INTERFACE_ENTRY(IParcel)
    COM_INTERFACE_ENTRY(IRelatedObjectEvents)
    COM_INTERFACE_ENTRY_AGGREGATE_BLIND(m_pInnerUnk)
END_COM_MAP()
```

Open the source code for the parcel (parcel.cpp). The method FinalConstruct is called by ATL as the final step of the COM class creation procedure. An instance of the feature COM class will be created in this method. Parcel holds a reference to the inner feature through the member variable m_pInnerUnk, a pointer to feature's IUnknown interface.

Also, a query interface is done to get a pointer to the only contained interface, IRelatedObjectEvents.

```
HRESULT Parcel::FinalConstruct()
{
  IUnknown * pOuter = GetControllingUnknown();

  if (FAILED
          (CoCreateInstance(__uuidof(Feature),
            /* create inner feature  */
            pOuter,
            CLSCTX_INPROC_SERVER,
            IID_IUnknown,
            (void**) &m_pInnerUnk)))
            /* hold it */
      return E_FAIL;
    // QI for IRelatedObjectEvents
    if (FAILED
            (m_pInnerUnk->
    QueryInterface(IID_IRelatedObjectEvents,
      (void**)&m_pIRelatedObjectEvents)))
      return E_FAIL;
    pOuter->Release();
    return S_OK;
}
```

Then stub code is created for methods of the local interface IParcel. All of them return E_NOTIMPL, as the developer has to provide the implementation. An example is the accessor for ParcelValue:

```
STDMETHODIMP Parcel::get_ParcelValue(long*
pParcelValue)
{
    return E_NOTIMPL;
}
```

And lastly, methods of the only contained interface, IRelatedObjectEvents, are created. An example is:

```
STDMETHODIMP
Parcel::RelatedObjectChanged(IRelationshipClass*
pRelationshipClass,
    IObject* pobjectThatChanged)
{
        return E_NOTIMPL;
}
```

Notice the methods you decided to override return E_NOTIMPL, while the others are just forwarding the call to the same interface implemented by the inner COM class.

It is in the implementation of these local and contained interfaces where the behavior of custom features is placed.

Although it might look a little intimidating at this point, the good news is all that stuff is already there! The CASE tools allow you to design your objects using a graphical language and then generate a lot of boilerplate code that takes care of a ton of details needed for the creation of custom features using C++. You can (almost) forget entirely about those details and concentrate on what you really want: writing the behavior of your custom features.

Inserting helper files

A couple of files containing helper functions were already in the source directory.

To add the files to the project:

1. Right-click the TutorialServer project and then click Add Files to Project.

2. Select the file databaseTools.h.

3. Repeat steps 1 and 2 to add the source file databaseTools.cpp.

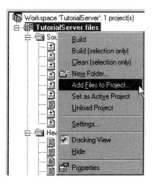

4. Double-click Building.cpp and add #include 'databaseTools.h' after the last #include in the file.

```
// Building.cpp : Implementation of Building
// Generated 9/22/99 11:28:15 AM
//
#include "stdafx.h"
#include "TutorialServer.h"
#include "Building.h"
#include "databaseTools.h"
```

5. Repeat step 4 for Parcel.cpp, ParcelClassExtension.cpp, and BuildingClassExtension.cpp.

Double-click databaseTools.cpp to open the source code. Two of the functions in databaseTools.cpp help you read and write values to and from fields in feature classes (GetFieldValue and PutFieldValue). The third function tells if a relationship class has a specific name (IsRelationshipClass).

Adding behavior for Building

We will start implementing the functionality of the Building feature. Open Building.cpp at this point. Only two methods require implementation, the accessor and mutator for the FieldValue property. This is the implementation of the methods:

```
                                 «interface»
  Building              «refines»  IBuilding
-Stories : esriFieldTypeInteger              -BuildingValue : long
-Height : esriFieldTypeInteger
-BuildingValue : esriFieldTypeInteger
-ParcelID : esriFieldTypeInteger
```

```
STDMETHODIMP Building::get_BuildingValue(long*
pBuildingValue)
{
    HRESULT      hr;
    CComBSTR     fieldName = L"BuildingValue";
    CComVariant value;

    IRowPtr      ipRow(GetControllingUnknown());
    if (ipRow == 0)
        return E_FAIL;
    if (FAILED
      (hr = GetFieldValue(fieldName, ipRow,
```

```
         &value)))
      return hr;

    *pBuildingValue = value.lVal;

    return hr;
}

STDMETHODIMP Building::put_BuildingValue(long
BuildingValue)
{
   CComBSTR    fieldName = L"BuildingValue";
   CComVariant value(BuildingValue);

   IRowPtr     ipRow(GetControllingUnknown());
   if (ipRow == 0)
      return E_FAIL;

   return PutFieldValue(fieldName, ipRow, value);
}
```

That completes the code for the building COM class. Now
we also want to create a custom validation rule that verifies
the height is at least the number of floors times 10 feet. The
code for the validation rule will be implemented inside the
class extension for the building. Open
BuildingClassExtension.cpp and insert code for the
ValidateRow method:

```
STDMETHODIMP
BuildingClassExtension::ValidateRow(IRow* pRow,
BSTR* pValidateRow)
{
   CComVariant height, stories;
   CComBSTR    bstrFieldName(L"Height");

   if (FAILED(GetFieldValue(bstrFieldName, pRow,
        &height)))
      return E_FAIL;

   bstrFieldName = L"Stories";

   if (FAILED(GetFieldValue(bstrFieldName, pRow,
        &stories)))
      return E_FAIL;

   CComBSTR bstrErrMsg;
   bstrErrMsg = L"The number of stories x 10ft
exceeds the building height";

   if (height.lVal < (stories.lVal * 10))
      *pValidateRow = bstrErrMsg.Copy();

   return S_OK;
}
```

When the user triggers the validation for a building this
code will be executed, and a message will be shown for
those buildings that are invalid.

Adding behavior for Parcel

Now let's go to the parcel. First, look at the code that keeps an eye on new buildings and creates relationships between the new building and the parcel containing it. This behavior is implemented in the Parcel class extension, which receives a notification each time a new related object is created. Open ParcelClassExtension.cpp and insert the following code as the implementation of the RelatedObjectCreated method.

```
STDMETHODIMP
ParcelClassExtension::RelatedObjectCreated(
        IRelationshipClass* pRelationshipClass,
        IObject* pobjectThatWasCreated)
{
  // first verify the relationship is
  // "Contains"
  if(!IsRelationshipClass
    (pRelationshipClass,CComBSTR(L"Contains")))
    return S_OK;

  // the relationship is "Contains", thus the
  // created object must be a building.

  IGeometryPtr ipBuildingGeometry;

  ((IFeaturePtr) pobjectThatWasCreated)->
  get_Shape(&ipBuildingGeometry);
```

```
  if (ipBuildingGeometry == 0)
      return E_FAIL;

  // Search for any parcel whose geometry
  // contains that of the newly created
  // building.

  IFeatureClassPtr
    ipParcelFeatureClass(m_pClass);
  IFeatureDatasetPtr    ipFeatureDataset;
  ISpatialReferencePtr ipSpatialReference;

  ipParcelFeatureClass->
   get_FeatureDataset(&ipFeatureDataset);
  ((IGeoDatasetPtr) ipFeatureDataset)->
   get_SpatialReference(&ipSpatialReference);

  // Prepare the spatial filter

  ISpatialFilterPtr
   ipSpatialFilter(CLSID_SpatialFilter);

   ipSpatialFilter->
      putref_Geometry(ipBuildingGeometry);
  ipSpatialFilter->
      put_SpatialRel(esriSpatialRelIntersects);
  CComBSTR shapeField(L"Shape");

  ipSpatialFilter->
      put_GeometryField(shapeField);
  ipSpatialFilter->
```

```
putref_OutputSpatialReference(shapeField,
 ipSpatialReference);
 // Do the query
HRESULT hr;
CComQIPtr<IParcel> ipParcel;
IFeatureCursorPtr ipParcels;

if (FAILED(hr = ipParcelFeatureClass->
    Search(ipSpatialFilter,
        VARIANT_FALSE,
        &ipParcels)))
 return hr;

// check a parcel was found

IFeaturePtr ipFeature;

if (ipParcels->NextFeature(&ipFeature) !=S_OK)
return S_OK;

ipParcel = ipFeature;

// Create an instance of the relationship.

IObjectClassPtr ipBuildingObjectClass;
IRelationshipPtr ipRelationship;

pobjectThatWasCreated->
    get_Class(&ipBuildingObjectClass);

return pRelationshipClass->
```

```
CreateRelationship((IObjectPtr) ipParcel,
                    pobjectThatWasCreated,
                    &ipRelationship);
}
```

The code first verifies the relationship class is 'Contains' because parcels could have relationships with other feature classes. Then it grabs the geometry of the object that was created (building) and searches for the parcel underneath it. If a parcel is found, a new contains relationship is created between the new building and the parcel.

Now let's go to the parcel object itself. Open Parcel.cpp at this point. We have two interfaces to implement: IParcel and IRelatedObjectEvents (the latter because we decided to contain it during code generation). The code behind the ParcelValue property and the read-only property CombinedBuildingValue is pretty much the same as the one used for the building value property.

```
STDMETHODIMP Parcel::get_ParcelValue(long*
pParcelValue)
{
    HRESULT    hr;
    CComBSTR   fieldName = L"ParcelValue";
    CComVariant value;

    IRowPtr    ipRow(GetControllingUnknown());
    if (ipRow == 0)
        return E_FAIL;
```

```
if (FAILED(hr = GetFieldValue(fieldName,
    ipRow, &value)))
    return hr;


*pParcelValue = value.lVal;


return hr;
}
STDMETHODIMP Parcel::put_ParcelValue(long
ParcelValue)
{
  CComBSTR    fieldName = L"ParcelValue";
  CComVariant value(ParcelValue);


  IRowPtr    ipRow(GetControllingUnknown());
  if (ipRow == 0)
    return E_FAIL;


  return PutFieldValue(fieldName, ipRow, value);
}
STDMETHODIMP
Parcel::get_CombinedBuildingValue(long*
pCombinedBuildingValue)
{
  HRESULT hr;
  CComBSTR  fieldName = "CombinedBuildingValue";
  CComVariant value;


  IRowPtr    ipRow(GetControllingUnknown());
  if (ipRow == 0)
    return E_FAIL;
```

```
if (FAILED(hr = GetFieldValue(fieldName,
    ipRow, &value)))
    return hr;


*pCombinedBuildingValue = value.lVal;


return hr;
}
```

The code for the last method of IParcel calculates the tax value of a parcel, based on a given tax rate, the parcel's value, and the combined value of the buildings in the parcel.

```
STDMETHODIMP Parcel::TaxValue(double TaxRate,
long* pTaxValue)
{
  // Dynamically calculate the tax value


  if (TaxRate < 0)
    return E_FAIL;


  long parcelValue, buildingValue;


  get_ParcelValue(&parcelValue);
  get_CombinedBuildingValue(&buildingValue);


  *pTaxValue = static_cast<long>((buildingValue
        + parcelValue) * TaxRate);


  return S_OK;
}
```

We want to keep the parcel's field CombinedBuildingValue updated if the value of a building changes or if a building is moved outside of a parcel. To implement this functionality, we will first create a couple of helper functions. The first function calculates the combined value of the buildings in a parcel. The second verifies a building is still contained in a parcel.

Open Parcel.h and insert the following prototypes in the private section of the class:

```
private:
  // helper functions
  HRESULT RecalculateCombinedBuildingValue(
          IRelationshipClass* pRelClass);
  HRESULT CheckBuildingContainment(
          IRelationshipClass* pRelClass,
          IObject* pBuildingObject);
```

Now open Parcel.cpp. The following routine maintains the combined building value updated. It loops through the related buildings calculating the total value. Then it writes the value to the database. Insert the code in your file.

```
HRESULT
Parcel::RecalculateCombinedBuildingValue(IRelationshipClass*
pRelClass)
{
  IRowPtr ipRow(GetControllingUnknown());
  if (ipRow == 0)
      return E_FAIL;

  HRESULT    hr;
  ISetPtr ipRelatedBuildings;
  if (FAILED(hr = pRelClass->
    GetObjectsRelatedToObject((IObjectPtr) ipRow,
                      &ipRelatedBuildings)))
    return hr;


  IRowPtr           ipBuildingRow;
  IUnknownPtr        ipUnk;
  CComQIPtr<IBuilding> ipBuilding;
  long              combinedBuildingValue = 0;

  while (ipRelatedBuildings->
    Next(&ipUnk) == S_OK)
    {
      long value;
      ipBuildingRow = ipUnk;
      ipBuilding = ipBuildingRow;
      ipBuilding->get_BuildingValue(&value);

      combinedBuildingValue += value;
    }

  // Persist the new combined building value.

  CComBSTR  fieldName = "CombinedBuildingValue";
  CComVariant value(combinedBuildingValue);

  if (FAILED(hr =
      PutFieldValue(fieldName, ipRow, value)))
      return hr;

      return ipRow->Store();
}
```

The second routine breaks the relationship between a building and a parcel if the building is moved and is no longer contained in the parcel. Notice that besides removing the relationship it also recalculates the combined building value.

```
HRESULT Parcel::CheckBuildingContainment(
            IRelationshipClass* pRelClass,
            IObject* pBuildingObject)
{
  // If the building is no longer contained
  // within the parcel, break the relationship
  // and recalculate the combined building
  // value.

  IFeaturePtr
    ipFeature(GetControllingUnknown());
  if (ipFeature == 0)
      return E_FAIL;

  IGeometryPtr ipBuildingGeometry,
    ipParcelGeometry;

  ((IFeaturePtr) pBuildingObject)->
  get_Shape(&ipBuildingGeometry);
    ipFeature->get_Shape(&ipParcelGeometry);

  VARIANT_BOOL contains;

  ((IRelationalOperatorPtr) ipParcelGeometry)->
    Contains(ipBuildingGeometry, &contains);

  if (contains == VARIANT_TRUE)
      return S_OK;

  // INVARIANT: The parcel no longer contains
  // the building.

  HRESULT hr;

  if (FAILED(hr = pRelClass->
    DeleteRelationship((IObjectPtr) ipFeature,
                            pBuildingObject)))
      return hr;
    return RecalculateCombinedBuildingValue
            (pRelClass);
}
```

Now let's work on the actual events received by the parcel through IRelatedObjectEvents. The first event is triggered when a single related object is changed. Either the shape or the value of one of its properties could have changed.

If the shape has changed, we test if the building is still contained within the parcel. If it is not contained we break the relationship and calculate the combined building value.

If the shape did not change, then perhaps the value of a building might have. In this case, we calculate the combined building value of the parcel.

Insert the following code as the implementation of the method RelatedObjectChanged.

```
STDMETHODIMP Parcel::RelatedObjectChanged(
        IRelationshipClass* pRelationshipClass,
        IObject* pobjectThatChanged)
{
  if (!pRelationshipClass ||
                        !pobjectThatChanged)
    return E_POINTER;

  if (!IsRelationshipClass(pRelationshipClass,
    CComBSTR(L"Contains")))
      return S_OK;

  HRESULT       hr;
  VARIANT_BOOL shapeChanged;
  IFeaturePtr  ipFeature(pobjectThatChanged);

  if (ipFeature == 0)
      return S_OK;

  IFeatureChangesPtr
      ipFeatureChanges(ipFeature);
  ipFeatureChanges->
      get_ShapeChanged(&shapeChanged);

  if (shapeChanged)
  {
    if (FAILED(hr = CheckBuildingContainment(
      pRelationshipClass, pobjectThatChanged)))
              return hr;
  }
    else
    {
      if (FAILED(hr =
        RecalculateCombinedBuildingValue
            (pRelationshipClass)))
          return hr;
    }

  return m_pIRelatedObjectEvents->
      RelatedObjectChanged(
                      pRelationshipClass,
                      pobjectThatChanged);
}
```

The second event we will handle is triggered when a set of buildings is moved. This case is a bit more complex because the geodata access components send this message only once to a parcel in the set of parcels whose buildings were moved. The parcel must handle the movement of its own buildings, remove itself from the set of affected parcels, and send the message to the next parcel in the set. Eventually, all parcels will handle the movement of their buildings.

In this implementation the parcel doesn't really remove itself from the affected parcels set. Instead, it creates a clone of the set and doesn't include itself in it. It is not fair to assume the routine can change the set passed in because the caller routine may use the set later on and would be really surprised to find an empty set.

Insert the following code as the implementation of the method RelatedObjectSetMoved.

```
STDMETHODIMP Parcel::RelatedObjectSetMoved(
      IRelationshipClass* pRelationshipClass,
      ISet*  pobjectsThatNeedToChange,
      ISet*  pobjectsThatChanged,
      ILine* pMoveVector)
{
  // check it is the Contains relationship
  if (!IsRelationshipClass
     (pRelationshipClass,CComBSTR(L"Contains")))
     return S_OK;

  IObjectPtr ipObject(GetControllingUnknown());
   if (ipObject == 0)
      return E_FAIL;

   // find the buildings related to the parcel

  ISetPtr ipRelatedBuildingObjects;

    pRelationshipClass->
                  GetObjectsRelatedToObject(
                  ipObject,
                  &ipRelatedBuildingObjects);
      pobjectsThatChanged->Reset();

  HRESULT      hr;
  ISetPtr      ipPrunedRelatedSet(CLSID_Set);
  IRowPtr      ipRelatedBuildingRow;
  IUnknownPtr  ipUnknown, ipUnkRelatedBuilding;
  IObjectPtr   ipRelatedBuildingObject;
```

```
// match buildings that changed to those
// really related to this parcel

while (pobjectsThatChanged->
   Next(&ipUnknown) == S_OK)
{
    bool matchFound = false;

    while (!matchFound &&
           ipRelatedBuildingObjects->
Next(&ipUnkRelatedBuilding) == S_OK)
    {

      if (ipUnknown == ipUnkRelatedBuilding)
         {
// building that changed found
// in the related buildings
// stop looking for it in the related
// buildings
         matchFound = true;

// check changed building is still contained
// by parcel
         ipRelatedBuildingObject = ipUnknown;
           if (FAILED(hr =
                 CheckBuildingContainment(
                 pRelationshipClass,
                 ipRelatedBuildingObject)))
             return hr;
      }
   }
```

```
}

// Clone the parcel set, removing self.

bool        remainingParcels = false;
ISetPtr     ipPrunedParcelSet(CLSID_Set);
IUnknownPtr ipUnkParcel, ipUnkSelf(ipObject);
IRelatedObjectEventsPtr ipNextParcel;

pobjectsThatNeedToChange->Reset();

while (pobjectsThatNeedToChange->
   Next(&ipUnkParcel) == S_OK)
{
   if (ipUnkParcel != ipUnkSelf)
    {
       remainingParcels = true;
       ipNextParcel = ipUnkParcel;
       ipPrunedParcelSet->Add(ipUnkParcel);
    }
}

if (!remainingParcels)
   return S_OK;

// Recursively call this method on one item
// in the cloned parcel set.
// If there are no remaining parcels,
// simply return.

return ipNextParcel->
```

```
RelatedObjectSetMoved(pRelationshipClass,
                      ipPrunedParcelSet,
                      ipPrunedRelatedSet,
                      pMoveVector);
}
```

We will leave other methods in the IRelatedObjectEvents untouched. They will be forwarded to the inner feature. However, some functionality is still to be developed for a fully functional model. For example, when a building is moved from one parcel to a different parcel, the relationship with the original parcel is broken, but the relationship with the new parcel is never created. As always, there is room for more development.

In Developer Studio, click the Build menu and then click Build TutorialServer.dll to compile the project. The library TutorialServer.dll will be created and registered in your system upon compilation.

Creating the schema

The second wizard of the CASE tools will help you create a schema for your UML models in a geodatabase. For each UML class in the model, a table will be created. For each UML attribute in the class, a field in the table will be created.

Depending on the parent class, an object class or a feature class is created. Object classes will be created for custom features that inherit from the Object class. Feature classes will be created for custom features inheriting from any other concrete class in the ESRI Classes Package. Feature classes can be further divided into simple feature classes—those inheriting from Feature, and network feature classes—those inheriting from junction or edge features. In the latter case a geometric network will be created as well.

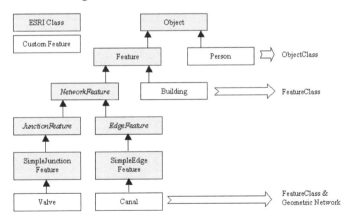

The wizard is a command in ArcCatalog. You can launch the wizard only when a feature dataset has been selected on the left-hand side panel of ArcCatalog. This implies the feature classes for custom features (and possibly a geometric network) will be created within that feature dataset.

To add the wizard command to ArcCatalog:

1. Start ArcCatalog.

2. Click Tools and then click Customize.

3. Click the Commands tab.

4. Click CASE tools in the categories list.

5. Drag the CASE tools command onto a toolbar.

6. Click Close.

   Note: The schema wizard can also be added to ArcCatalog as an entry in the context menu for feature datasets. See *Building a Geodatabase*.

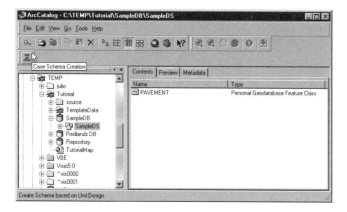

Overview of the schema creation

You will create a schema for the tutorial model. Under a selected feature dataset, the wizard will create two feature classes (building and parcel) and a composite relationship class (contains). The wizard will guide you through the following steps:

- Connect to the Repository.
- Select the object model.
- Select the custom features for which schema will be created.
- Define schema properties for each selected custom feature.
- Create the schema.

To start the wizard select the geodatabase and feature dataset you want to use as a target for the creation of the schema (for example, C:\Tutorial\SampleDB\SampleDS). Selecting the dataset should enable the Schema Wizard button.

Creating the schema

The first three steps are exactly the same as those of the Code Generation Wizard, described previously. Start the wizard, connect to the repository, and select the tutorial model now.

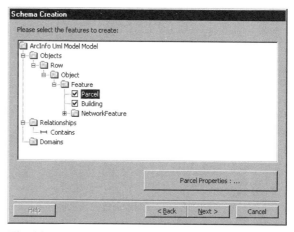

The hierarchy of the model shown by the schema wizard is similar to that shown by the code generation wizard. However, besides showing the custom features, it also shows relationship classes and domains. Click the plus sign by the Objects folder to expand the hierarchy and double-click parcel to open its properties.

This dialog shows the properties of the feature class that will be created including geometry type, fields, relationships, and behavior COM classes. Notice Polygon is selected in the geometry type dropdown menu, because it was specified as a tagged value of the corresponding parcel UML class in the model.

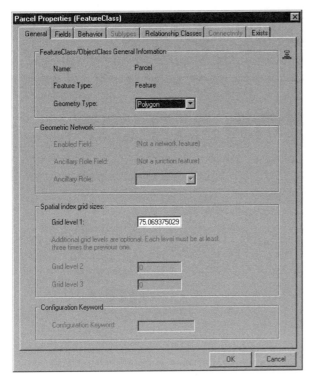

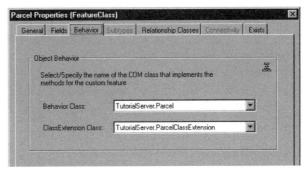

Scroll down in the hierarchy and expand the Relationships folder to see the relationship classes in the model. Double-click contains to open the properties dialog. Notice all the information is read directly from the association in the UML model including notification and primary and foreign keys. Click OK to dismiss the dialog and then Click Next to continue with the wizard.

Click the Behavior tab and notice the parcel custom feature and the associated class extension have been selected automatically. The schema wizard looks for the Behavior COM classes in the system's registry, and therefore it is necessary to register the Dynamic Link Library beforehand (compiling in Developer Studio registered the TutorialServer.dll). Click OK to dismiss the dialog.

Use the same procedure to verify the definition of the Building feature class. Check that the geometry type and behavior classes have been correctly read from the model.

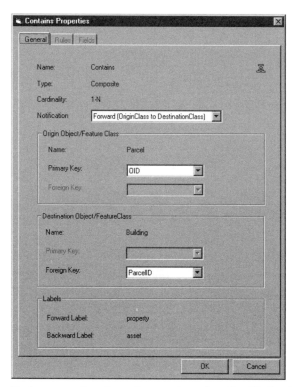

Before creating the schema, the wizard will display a summary of the custom features and options you selected. Click Finish to create the schema.

Verifying the schema

In ArcCatalog, double-click the SampleDS feature dataset to refresh the list of feature classes in it. Notice the two polygon feature classes have been added along with the contains relationship class.

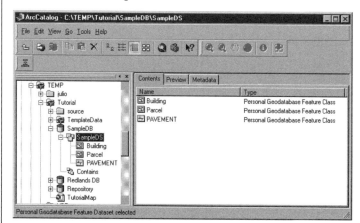

Double-click the parcel feature class to open the properties dialog. Click the Fields tab and notice the fields correspond to those defined in the UML model for the parcel class. The fields shape_length and shape_area are automatically added and maintained by the geodata access components for any polygon feature class. Click OK to close the dialog.

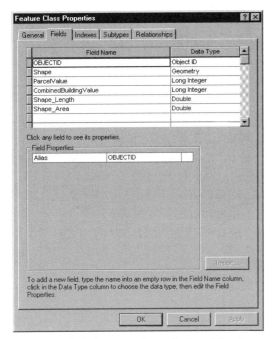

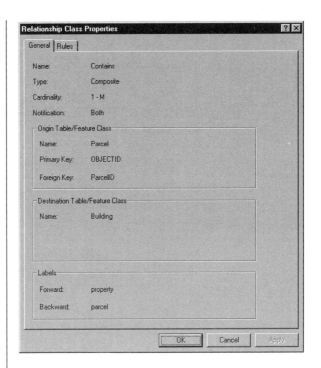

Double-click the contains relationship class and verify the
properties, as seen by ArcCatalog. When done, click OK to
dismiss the dialog.

Using the custom features in ArcMap

In this section of the tutorial, you'll create a few parcels and buildings to test the schema and the functionality implemented in the Behavior COM classes.

Start ArcMap and drag and drop the SampleDS feature dataset from ArcCatalog onto ArcMap. Make sure the Editor toolbar is available. Save the map as TutorialMap in the Tutorial folder.

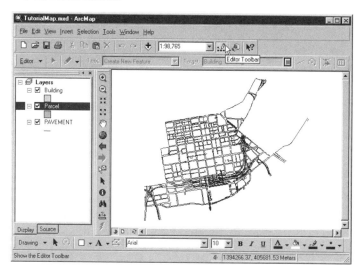

Testing the custom feature behavior

You will create a couple of parcels and buildings in this step. Zoom in to a single block in the map to create the parcels.

1. In the Editor toolbar select Editor and then click Start Editing.

2. Verify the current Task is Create New Feature, Click the Target dropdown arrow and then click Parcel.

3. Click the Create New Feature tool and then use the mouse to digitize two parcels.

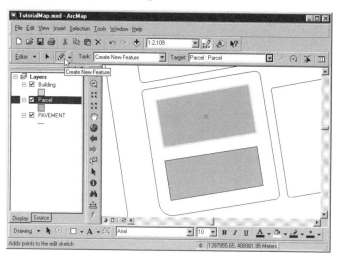

Now you'll create the buildings. Click the Target dropdown arrow and click Building. Digitize two buildings inside a parcel. With a building selected, click the Attributes tool to open the Property Inspector. Click the plus sign by the building ID and notice it has a related parcel. The relationship was created by the Parcel class extension in response to the creation of a related object, the building.

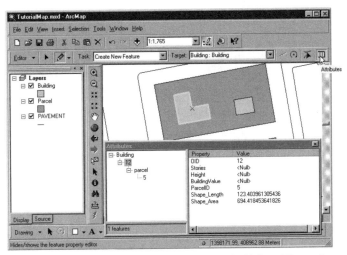

In the Property Inspector click the first building ID again and fill in values for the fields as indicated in the following table:

Field	Value
Stories	1
Height	12
BuildingValue	50,000

Select the second building in the parcel and specify the following attributes:

Field	Value
Stories	1
Height	8
BuildingValue	10,000

The parcel custom feature recalculates the combined building value each time a related building field value changes. In the map, select the parcel to display its attributes. Notice how the current combined building value is 60,000, the sum of the value of the two buildings. The parcel itself does not have a value yet, so change the parcel value to 45,000.

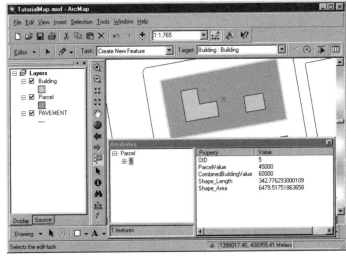

Close the Attributes dialog and select the two buildings in the parcel. Click the Editor menu and then click Validate Selection to verify the selected buildings. For one of the buildings the number of stories is 1 and the height is 8, which violates the custom validation rule implemented in the building class extension. Click OK to dismiss the message.

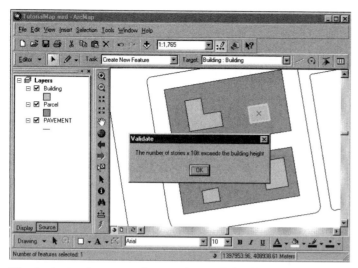

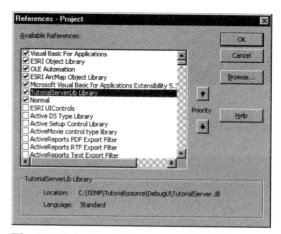

The last step is to use the services of the IParcel interface programmatically, specifically the calculation of the tax value given a tax rate. We will create a Visual Basic for Applications (VBA) macro that loops through the selected features, asks for the IParcel interface, and uses the method.

To create the VBA macro

1. In the Tools menu, select Macros and then Visual Basic Editor.

2. In the Visual Basic Editor, select Tools and then click References.

3. Scroll down and select the TutorialServerLib Library as a reference.

The tutorial server library provides Visual Basic with the types inside the TutorialServer.dll created with ATL/C++. Types such as IParcel or Parcel are defined there.

4. Click OK to accept changes to the references.

5. In the Project Explorer, click the plus sign by the 'Project(TutorialMap.mxd)'.

6. Click the plus sign by ArcMap Objects.

7. Double-click ThisDocument.

8. Copy the following code:

```
Public Sub ParcelInformation()
   Dim pDoc As IMxDocument
   Dim pMap As IMap
   Dim pLayer As ILayer
   Dim pFeatLayer As IFeatureLayer
   Dim pFeatSelection As IFeatureSelection
   Dim pSelectionSet As ISelectionSet
   Dim pRow As IRow
   Dim pCursor As ICursor
```

```
Dim pParcel As IParcel
Dim sMsg As String
Dim nTotal As Long

Set pDoc = ThisDocument
Set pMap = pDoc.FocusMap
Set pLayer = pDoc.SelectedLayer

If pLayer Is Nothing Then
  MsgBox "Please select the parcel layer", _
  vbInformation
  Exit Sub
End If

Set pFeatLayer = pLayer
Set pFeatSelection = pFeatLayer
Set pSelectionSet = _
 pFeatSelection.SelectionSet

pSelectionSet.Search Nothing, True, pCursor
Set pRow = pCursor.NextRow
If pRow Is Nothing Then MsgBox _
    "Please select a parcel", vbInformation

 Do While Not pRow Is Nothing
   sMsg = ""
   If TypeOf pRow Is IParcel Then
     Set pParcel = pRow
     nTotal = _
         pParcel.CombinedBuildingValue + _
         pParcel.ParcelValue
```

```
        sMsg = "Buildings plus parcel : " & _
        nTotal & vbNewLine
        sMsg = sMsg & _
        "Tax Value (rate = 0.25) : " & _
        pParcel.TaxValue(0.25)
        MsgBox sMsg, vbInformation, _
        "Parcel Information"
     End If
     Set pRow = pCursor.NextRow
   Loop
 End Sub
```

The macro first finds the selected layer. Then it loops through the selected features and tries to get the IParcel interface. If successful, it uses the interface on the current parcel to get the tax value and report it to the user.

In ArcMap, use the Customize dialog to add the macro to a toolbar. Select the parcel layer and then select the parcel with buildings. Click the button you added to run the macro's code.

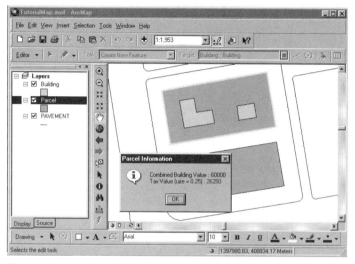

To see the results of the rest of your work, try the following.

In ArcMap, start editing again, select the parcel with buildings, and move it. The buildings move with the parcel.

Select a building and move it outside the parcel. Select the parcel and open the Property Inspector. Notice that the combined building value has changed for the parcel.

In the Editor menu, select Stop Editing and then answer Yes to save your edits.

Building and delivering extensions

Without realizing it, you may have already worked with extensions, packages of additional functionality assembled from one or more COM components, in either ArcCatalog or ArcMap. These include the Metadata extension in ArcCatalog and the Editor and the UtilityNetworkAnalysis extensions in ArcMap. ArcCatalog, ArcMap, the Editor, and many other parts of ArcInfo are designed to host additional extensions. Extensions are important to end-users because they can control what pieces of functionality are installed on a machine or loaded at run time. The key benefit to developers is that ArcInfo provides standard mechanisms for plugging extensions and other components into the system. This chapter contains information about building extensions and delivering extensions and other includes some example code useful when integrated with external setup programs.

What is an extension?

What functionality your extension provides is up to you. An extension might, for example, initiate a customization filter or provide automatic feature validation within an edit session or provide a toolbar with tools that are available when specific data exists, and so on. You can register your extension with the existing extension. An extension is a component or set of components that does two things. First, it implements an interface that is expected by the application. And second, it registers itself with the application so that it may be loaded at the appropriate time. Both the interface that it implements and the mechanism it uses to register itself depend on what type of extension it is. Usually, the mechanism used to register a type of extension is a component category. Component categories identify those areas of functionality that a software component supports and requires; a registry entry is used for each category or identified area of functionality. Extensions become part of the application once they've been registered in the appropriate component category. A globally unique identifier (GUID) identifies each component category. The application, Categories.exe, located in the <installation directory>\bin folder, provides a user interface for registration of extensions, and for that matter, other areas of the system that use the extension mechanism such as Renderers and GX Views.

Creating an extension

Many of the extension types in ArcInfo rely on the IExtension interface. You create one of these extensions simply by implementing IExtension. Once you've registered the extension with the appropriate category, the application becomes aware of it and can manage its lifetime. That is, the Editor or ArcMap or ArcCatalog will create your extension object on startup and release it on shutdown. Once the system creates the extension, you can do anything you want—listen for and respond to events, provide additional user interface elements, load additional components, and so on.

How To

In order to create an extension, you should write code to do the following:

1. Create a class that will allow you to implement the appropriate extension interface. In this class you'll implement the methods of the IExtension interface. ▶

```
Option Explicit
Implements IExtension            ①
' This custom editor extension validates features whenever they are
' created or modified. This is accomplished by creating an editor
' extension that listens for the events IEditEvents::OnChangeFeature and
' IEditEvents::OnCreateFeature.
' Validation requires validation rules; i.e., connectivity rules,
' relationships rules, or attribute domains.


Private m_pEditor As IEditor
Private WithEvents m_pEditorEvents As esriCore.Editor
Private m_pFeature As IFeature


Private Property Get IExtension_Name() As String    ②
    IExtension_Name = "Custom Editor Extension"
End Property

                                                    ④

Private Sub IExtension_Shutdown()     ⑤
    Set m_pEditor = Nothing
    Set m_pEditorEvents = Nothing
End Sub


Private Sub IExtension_Startup(initializationData As Variant)   ③
    'initializationData is a variant which in this case is
    'the Editor object
    Set m_pEditor = initializationData
    Set m_pEditorEvents = m_pEditor
End Sub
```

2. Give the extension a name. This lets you distinguish the extension from others.

3. Set the context and any other initializations for the extension on startup.

4. Perform operations in response to events.

5. Release objects on shutdown.

```
Private Sub m_pEditorEvents_OnChangeFeature(ByVal obj As  ④
esriCore.IObject)
    'Call Validate whenever a feature is modified
    Set m_pFeature = obj
    Validate m_pFeature 'obj is an IFeature
End Sub

Private Sub m_pEditorEvents_OnCreateFeature(ByVal obj As  ④
esriCore.IObject)
    'Call Validate whenever a feature is created
    Set m_pFeature = obj
    Validate m_pFeature 'obj is an IFeature
End Sub

Private Sub Validate(pFeature As IFeature)
    'Validate the feature passed in
    Dim pValidate As IValidate
    Dim ErrorMessage As String
    Dim isValid As Boolean
    Set pValidate = pFeature
    isValid = True 'Assume feature is valid
    isValid = pValidate.Validate(ErrorMessage)
    'Only display a message if the feature is invalid
    'Don't use the ErrorMessage for anything in this sample
    If Not isValid Then
        MsgBox "Invalid Feature"
    End If
End Sub
```

Registering an extension by hand

If you've created an extension for your own use or within a work group, you may decide that the easiest way to make the extension available is to provide instructions for registering the extension by hand. You'll work with the utility program, Categories.exe, that's located in the <installation directory>\bin folder.

1. Move to the <installation directory>\bin folder and run Categories.exe.

2. In the Component Category Manager, double-click the category with which you want to register the extension.

3. Click Add Object.

4. In the Find Add-In dialog navigate to the extension, select it, and then click Open.

5. In the Add Objects dialog check all objects to be added to the component category.

6. Click OK.

   The Component Category Manager dialog displays the extension that you've added.

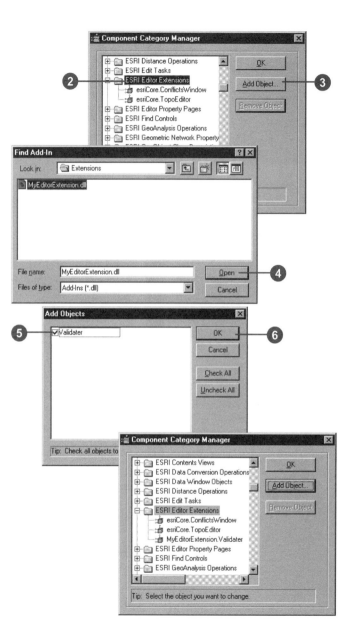

Registering an extension with code

If you plan to distribute an extension to a wider audience or as a commercial third party product, you may decide to create an installation program for the DLL. Creating an install program ensures that your extension will be placed in the proper location and may help to minimize support calls. You can create an executable that handles the registration of the extension in the appropriate component categories and integrate it with the rest of the installation program.

Tip

Register the extension first
Before invoking the Setup or SetupObject method, make sure to register the DLL that represents the extension.

How To

In order to register an extension, you should write code to do the following:

1. Establish the GUID of the extension and the component category in which it will be registered.

   Run Regedit.exe and search for the name of the extension you created. You can start your search in HKEY_CLASSES_ROOT\CLSID. Record the GUID. Then search for the name of the component category and record its GUID, too.

2. Create a ComponentCategoryManager object and UID objects.

3. Set the value of the UID objects to the GUID for the category and the GUID for the extension.

4. Specify the location of the extension DLL.

   The location is where the DLL will reside on the local machine. Use a pathname that avoids folder names with spaces.

```
Private Sub RegisterExtension()

    Const Extension_Category As Variant = _     ①
    "{58122E51-D89C-11D2-9F25-00C04F6BC979}"
    Const My_Extension As Variant = _
    "{98C7FB59-8513-11D3-816D-000000000000}"

    Dim pCCMgr As IComponentCategoryManager    ②
    Dim sDLLName As String
    Dim pCatGUID As New esriCore.UID
    Dim pExtGUID As New esriCore.UID

    Set pCCMgr = New ComponentCategoryManager
    pCatGUID.Value = Extensions_Category       ③
    pExtGUID.Value = My_Extension
    sDLLName = _                               ④
    "C:\Winnt\System32\MyEditorExtension.dll"
    pCCMgr.SetupObject sDLLName, pExtGUID, _   ⑤
    pCatGUID,True

End Sub
```

Tip

Registering more than one object

IComponentCategoryManager's Setup method provides a means of registering more than one object stored in a DLL. Setup will QI each object in the DLL for the interface objectType; if the QI succeeds it will add that object to the component category specified by the category parameter.

Tip

If you're building a C++ component

Add logic to your self-registration code to register in the component category.

5. Invoke the SetupObject method.

SetupObject will register one specific object into a component category. It will find the object that has the GUID that matches the specified extension object UID and add that object to the component category specified by the category UID parameter.

Selected GUID values

Component Category	GUID
ESRI Editor Extensions	"{58122E51-D89C-11D2-9F25-00C04F6BC979}"
ESRI Edit Tasks	"{58122E50-D89C-11D2-9F25-00C04F6BC979}"
ESRI GeoObjects	"{D4E2A321-5D59-11D2-89FD-006097AFF44E}"
ESRI Gx CommandBars	"{56C205F9-E53A-11D1-9496-080009EEBECB}"
ESRI Gx Commands	"{5F08CBCA-E91F-11D1-AEE8-080009EC734B}"
ESRI Gx Extensions	"{4531C69D-DC07-11D2-9F2F-00C04F6BC69E}"
ESRI GX Extension Toolbars	"{58374DA9-3A52-11D3-9F70-00C04F6BC69E}"
ESRI Mx CommandBars	"{B56A7C4A-83D4-11D2-A2E9-080009B6F22B}"
ESRI Mx Commands	"{B56A7C42-83D4-11D2-A2E9-080009B6F22B}"
ESRI Mx Extensions	"{B56A7C45-83D4-11D2-A2E9-080009B6F22B}"
ESRI Property Pages	"{C899AE27-E515-11D1-877C-0000F8751720}"

Registering an extension with a registry file

Using a registry (.reg) file is a simple and effective way to register an extension in its appropriate component category. In addition to registering extensions, this technique is useful for registering any other components you create, such as commands or tools, freeing the user from having to register the command with the Add from file button in the Commands tab of the Customize dialog box.

Another benefit of using registry files is that they are fully supported within Visual Basic's Package and Deployment Wizard, a tool that helps you create installation packages for your Visual Basic applications and install them to your end-users' computers.

How To

Open a text file and add the appropriate information. Save the file with a .reg file extension.

```
REGEDIT4
// Sample registry file showing how to add an extension
// to two component categories
//
// {B56A7C42-83D4-11d2-A2E9-080009B6F22B} MxCommands CATID
// {B56A7C45-83D4-11d2-A2E9-080009B6F22B} MxExtensions CATID

// {302AA084-4A92-11D3-9F39-00C04F8ECE3A} MapProductionExtensions CLSID

// Add it to the MxCommands Component Category
// (the following three lines should all be on one line)
[HKEY_LOCAL_MACHINE\SOFTWARE\Classes\CLSID\{302AA084-4A92-11D3-9F39-
00C04F8ECE3A}
\Implemented Categories\{B56A7C42-83D4-11d2-A2E9-080009B6F22B}]
//
// Add it to the MxExtensions Component Category
// (the following three lines should all be on one line)
[HKEY_LOCAL_MACHINE\SOFTWARE\Classes\CLSID\{302AA084-4A92-11D3-9F39-
00C04F8ECE3A}
\Implemented Categories\{B56A7C45-83D4-11d2-A2E9-080009B6F22B}]
```

Working with the Package and Deployment Wizard

If you have Visual Basic 6.0, you can use its Package and Deployment Wizard to install extensions or other components and make use of the Wizard's registry file support to properly register them in the appropriate component categories. Other installation script software may support similar functionality.

This section describes only a portion of the Package and Deployment Wizard work flow. It covers the steps to take to include a registry file in a package. Consult the Wizard's Help for information about the other dialogs. Note that you can install an extension or other component to any location on disk. As long as it is properly registered in the appropriate component category, its functionality will be available.

Including a registry file in a package

1. In the Included Files dialog, click Add.

2. Navigate to the folder containing the registry file you want to add to the package.

3. Specify Registry Files (*.reg) in the Files of type combobox.

4. Double-click the registry file.

5. Click Next.

6. In the Registry Information dialog make sure that the Update Registry option is set to Yes. This will run the registry file as part of your installation. If you want you can also set the Copy File option to Yes to copy the registry file to the user's computer.

7. Click Next and proceed with the rest of the Wizard.

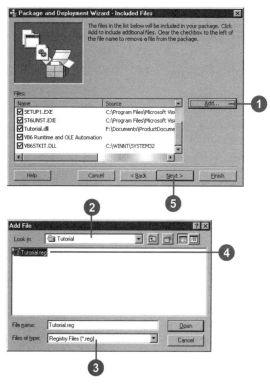

If you are a Visual C++ developer using ATL, you have the option of using a macro inside your code that, when compiled, will add all the extension or component registration code to the compiled DLL. This macro should be placed in the header file for the COM class implementing the interfaces.

```
// macro to be placed in the header file for the COM class
// implementing the interfaces; here, HospitalUnit is the name of the
// class that implements the functionality.
BEGIN_CATEGORY_MAP(HospitalUnit)
  IMPLEMENTED_CATEGORY(CATID_MxExtensions)
  IMPLEMENTED_CATEGORY(CATID_MxCommands)
END_CATEGORY_MAP()



// The header file for the Mx CATIDs
// {B56A7C42-83D4-11d2-A2E9-080009B6F22B}
DEFINE_GUID(CATID_MxCommands,
0xb56a7c42, 0x83d4, 0x11d2, 0xa2, 0xe9, 0x8, 0x0, 0x9, 0xb6, 0xf2, 0x2b);

// {B56A7C43-83D4-11d2-A2E9-080009B6F22B}
DEFINE_GUID(CATID_MxViewCommands,
0xb56a7c43, 0x83d4, 0x11d2, 0xa2, 0xe9, 0x8, 0x0, 0x9, 0xb6, 0xf2, 0x2b);

// {B56A7C44-83D4-11d2-A2E9-080009B6F22B}
DEFINE_GUID(CATID_GeoElementTools,
0xb56a7c44, 0x83d4, 0x11d2, 0xa2, 0xe9, 0x8, 0x0, 0x9, 0xb6, 0xf2, 0x2b);

// {B56A7C45-83D4-11d2-A2E9-080009B6F22B}
DEFINE_GUID(CATID_MxExtension,
0xb56a7c45, 0x83d4, 0x11d2, 0xa2, 0xe9, 0x8, 0x0, 0x9, 0xb6, 0xf2, 0x2b);

// {B56A7C46-83D4-11d2-A2E9-080009B6F22B}
DEFINE_GUID(CATID_PrinterPropertySheet,
0xb56a7c46, 0x83d4, 0x11d2, 0xa2, 0xe9, 0x8, 0x0, 0x9, 0xb6, 0xf2, 0x2b);
```

▶

```
// {B56A7C47-83D4-11d2-A2E9-080009B6F22B}
DEFINE_GUID(CATID_ExporterPropertySheet,
0xb56a7c47, 0x83d4, 0x11d2, 0xa2, 0xe9, 0x8, 0x0, 0x9, 0xb6, 0xf2, 0x2b);

// {B56A7C48-83D4-11d2-A2E9-080009B6F22B}
DEFINE_GUID(CATID_MxPalettes,
0xb56a7c48, 0x83d4, 0x11d2, 0xa2, 0xe9, 0x8, 0x0, 0x9, 0xb6, 0xf2, 0x2b);

// {B56A7C49-83D4-11d2-A2E9-080009B6F22B}
DEFINE_GUID(CATID_DataWindowFactory,
0xb56a7c49, 0x83d4, 0x11d2, 0xa2, 0xe9, 0x8, 0x0, 0x9, 0xb6, 0xf2, 0x2b);

// {B56A7C4A-83D4-11d2-A2E9-080009B6F22B}
DEFINE_GUID(CATID_MxCommandBars,
0xb56a7c4a, 0x83d4, 0x11d2, 0xa2, 0xe9, 0x8, 0x0, 0x9, 0xb6, 0xf2, 0x2b);

// {DF933391-7A7A-11d2-ACF9-0000F87808EE}
DEFINE_GUID(CATID_PrinterDrivers,
0xdf933391, 0x7a7a, 0x11d2, 0xac, 0xf9, 0x0, 0x0, 0xf8, 0x78, 0x8, 0xee);

// {5FDE0991-7B12-11d2-ACF9-0000F87808EE}
DEFINE_GUID(CATID_ExporterDrivers,
0x5fde0991, 0x7b12, 0x11d2, 0xac, 0xf9, 0x0, 0x0, 0xf8, 0x78, 0x8, 0xee);

// {8803C8EF-75FE-11d3-A6A6-0008C7D3AE50}
DEFINE_GUID(CATID_MxFinders,
0x8803c8ef, 0x75fe, 0x11d3, 0xa6, 0xa6, 0x0, 0x8, 0xc7, 0xd3, 0xae, 0x50);
```

▶

```
// {52BB5364-947E-11d2-ACFF-0000F87808EE}
DEFINE_GUID(CATID_ClipboardFormats,
0x52bb5364, 0x947e, 0x11d2, 0xac, 0xff, 0x0, 0x0, 0xf8, 0x78, 0x8, 0xee);

// {5BF495FA-95D1-11D2-AAEB-00C04FA37D59};
DEFINE_GUID(CATID_TraceTasks,
0x5bf495fa, 0x95d1, 0x11d2, 0xaa, 0xeb, 0x0, 0xc0, 0x4f, 0xa3, 0x7d,
0x59);

// {289C9956-C063-11d2-9F22-00C04F6BC8DD}
DEFINE_GUID(CATID_Pictures,
0x289c9956, 0xc063, 0x11d2, 0x9f, 0x22, 0x0, 0xc0, 0x4f, 0x6b, 0xc8,
0xdd);

// {089874FC-CC18-11d2-9F39-00C04F6BC78E}
DEFINE_GUID(CATID_ContentsViews,
0x89874fc, 0xcc18, 0x11d2, 0x9f, 0x39, 0x0, 0xc0, 0x4f, 0x6b, 0xc7, 0x8e);
```

Index

M

M-values 151
  setting 153
Macro items 83
Macro viruses 52
Macros 42, 67
  adding to toolbars 44
  and customizations 85–86
  creating 42
  editing 42
  running
    from Macros dialog box 43
    from module 43
Main Menu 24
Map layers
  accessing 103
Map units
  converting to 18
Map-to-page transformation 110
Maps property 102, 103
MapsChanged event 80
Measure values 151
Menu items 82
  described 24
Menus
  adding to toolbars 29
  described 24
Methods 62
  overriding 187
Microsoft Repository
  connecting to 181
Microsoft Visual Basic for Applications 2
Modal forms 69
Modeless forms 69
Models
  creating 168
  exporting to Repository 179
Modules 66, 68, 70
  class 68
Mouse dragging operations 109

Mouse events
  responding with SelectionTracker 110
MultiItem 83
MultiItems
  creating 94–95
MultiPoint objects 151
Multiuser editing
  rules 145–146
MxDocument 81, 102
  OnContextMenu event 87
  OpenDocument event 100
MxDocument object 102

N

Name objects 142
  benefits of 142
  types of 142
Network connectivity rules 143
Networks 143
New map document dialog 40
New Menu command 29
NewDocument event 80
NewDocument method 102
NextFeature method 144
NextRow method 144
Normal template 25, 52, 66, 78
Normal.gxt 67, 78, 81
  regenerating 40
Normal.mxt 25, 66, 78, 81
  regenerating 40
Nothing keyword 56, 144

O

Object Browser 21, 61
Object libraries 42, 60
  referencing 15
Object model
  ArcCatalog 134
  ArcMap 102–104

Object model (continued)
  Customization Framework 81–84
  Display 109–110
  Editor 118–121
  Geodatabase 142–146
  Geometry 151–152
  Output 132
  Spatial reference 158–160
Object models
  creating with Visio 168
  selecting 181
Object references 61–62
Objects 54
  as parameters 63–64
OnContextMenu event 80, 87
Online help 3
OpenDocument event 80, 100, 102
OpenFeatureClass method 106
OpenFromFile method
  code example 105
Operations
  defined 173
Out-of-process servers 54
Outbound interfaces 56

P

Package and Deployment Wizard 216, 217
Packages 168
  and diagrams 169
  registry files 217
Page layout views
  and PageLayout objects 102
PageLayout object 103
Panning 102, 110
Paper objects 132
Parameters
  defined 174
Path objects 151
Personal geodatabase (Access)
  adding data 106

Point objects 151
Polygon objects 151
Polygons
    and Ring objects 151
Polyline objects 151
Polylines 153
Polymorphism 55, 146
PrintDocument method 102
Printer objects 132
Procedure stubs 16
Procedures 68
    adding to module 68
ProgIDs 59
Project
    primary document filename 78
ProjectedCoordinateSystem coclass 159
    code example 163–164
Projects
    locking 70
    VBA 66–67
ProjectTemplate
    base template file name 78
Properties 62, 68
PropertySets 143
    and SDE workspaces 143
ProportionalSymbolRender coclass 109
Protection tab 70

Q

Query filters
    and '*' 145
QueryFilters 143–144
    and feature cursors 143
QueryInterface method 56
    and Implements 73
    and Visual Basic 57–58

R

Range domains 142, 177
RasterLayer coclass 103
Rasters
    as type of Name object 142
Reference counting 56
References dialog box 73
Registry 59
Registry files 216
    including in packages 217
Relational operators 151
Relationship rules 143, 177
RelationshipClasses 143
    as type of Name object 142
    creating 175–177
Release method 56
Remove command 70
Removing project items 70
Renderers 109
Repository
    connecting to 181
Repository.mdb 166
Resetting
    commands 35
Retrieving data 144
Ring objects 151
Rows 143
Rules
    kinds of 177
Running code 71–72

S

SampleDB.mdb 166
Save in combo box 31, 79
Saving 70
    a map as a template 39
ScaleDependentRenderer coclass 109
Schema
    creating 199–201
    verifying 201–202

Schema creation 198–202
    overview 199
Schema generation 166
Schema wizard
    adding to ArcCatalog 198
Scope 78
Scroll bars
    hiding 6–7
    showing 6–7
SDE databases
    and SQL where clause 144
SDE workspaces
    and PropertySets 143
    creating 147
Search cursors
    nonrecycling 145
Searching data 143–144
Security 52
Segments 156
SelectionChange event
    UIComboBoxControl 83
Servers 54–55
SetDomain method 158
Shapefiles
    adding 105
    and SQL where clause 144
ShapefileWorkspaceFactory coclass
    code example 105
Shortcut keys
    assigning 36
    contrasted with access keys 36
    creating 36
    removing 37
    resetting 38
Shortcut menus
    creating 87
ShowStartup
    registry entry 108
Sketch operations 119–120
Smooth method 151
Snap agents 120
    creating 125